★ ★ ★ ★ Battle of Nashville Preservation Society

MW00637163

Guide to
CIVIL WAR
NASHVILLE

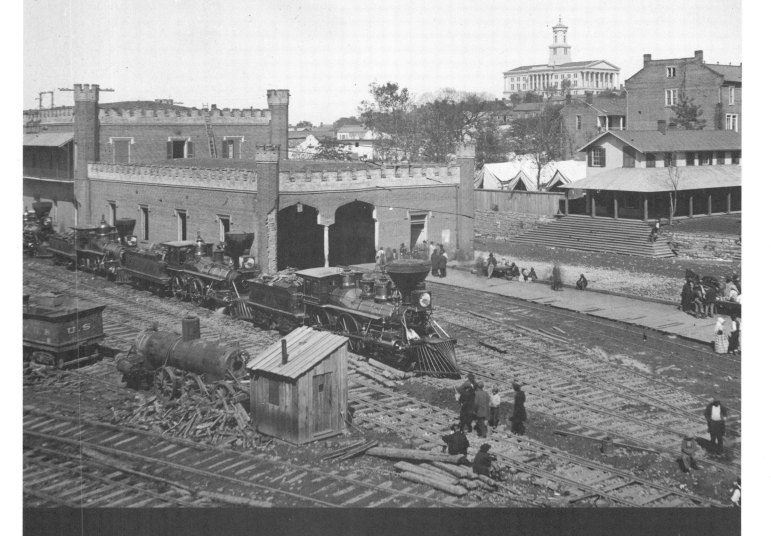

Mark Zimmerman

Table of Contents

Published by the Battle of Nashville Preservation Society, P.O. Box 190493, Nashville, TN 37219-0493

ISBN 0-9747236-0-6

Cover photographs courtesy of the Library of Congress and the Tennessee State Library and Archives.

Thanks to Ross Massey and George Gause for editorial assistance.

Printed in the USA by Lithographics, Inc., Nashville, TN.

For purchase information, visit the BONPS website at www.bonps.org.

Civil War Nashville

Nashville, Tennessee on the bluffs of the Cumberland River was the most cosmopolitan city west of the mountains, second only to New Orleans. In 1850, it hosted the convention on Southern secession. Ten years later, it was considered for the capital of the Confederacy. In early 1862, Nashville became the first Confederate state capital to fall to Union troops, surrendered without firing a shot. The pro-Confederate citizenry remained under tight Federal military rule until the end of the war more than three years later. During that time, the U.S. Army developed the city into a major transportation hub and supply depot to support the military campaigns against Chattanooga in 1863 and against Atlanta in 1864. In defense against numerous real and imagined Confederate cavalry and guerilla attacks, Nashville was transformed into the most heavily fortified city in North America, second only to Washington, D.C. From 1862-65, the population of Nashville increased threefold, and included a frightened yet defiant citizenry, an obsessed military governor, garrison soldiers and transient troops, merchants, teamsters, machinists, laborers, refugees, runaway slaves, hospital patients, prisoners of war, military police, doctors and nurses, prostitutes, pickpockets, smugglers, highwaymen, lawyers, agents of opportunity, sutlers, drunks, sailors, cavalrymen, spies, freedmen, and others. Late in the war, the weary Army of Tennessee marched north from Georgia to retake the capital of its namesake state, terrifying war officials in Washington, only to be crushed by an overwhelming hodgepodge of blueclad troops. Arguably the most decisive battle of the war, the Battle of Nashville ended major military activity in the Western Theater. Thusly, the Army of Northern Virginia could not be reinforced. In four months, the war was over. A civilian government was re-established at Nashville. A year after that, Tennessee became the first state to be re-admitted back into the Union.

How to Use The Tour Guide

There is no battlefield park at Nashville. The field of battle, one of the largest of the war, was lost long ago to urban development. There are, however, several remnants which have been preserved. The driving tour consists of 25 sites on a 50-mile route which can be customized to suit each visitor's time considerations. The full route, including stops and guided tours, will consume a full day of activity.

The route will take you through the downtown area, commercial districts, low-income districts, and affluent neighborhoods. Please pay attention to traffic and street signage and please respect the private property of others.

Maps of the driving tour can be found on pages 38-39, followed by driving instructions and the text of the Battle of Nashville historical markers. Due to various factors, many of these markers cannot be located or examined closely. Also, please bear in mind that street routes and designations can change. Road construction may also affect the driving route. Please be alert to hazards and drive carefully!

Two National Historic Landmarks are included on the tour—the State Capitol and the Downtown Presbyterian Church. The State Museum is nearby and free for visitors. Brochures and other touring information can be obtained at the city's Visitors Center.

Those interested in antebellum homes will find three such house museums on the tour—Belmont, Travellers Rest, and Belle Meade—all of which feature guided tours. Three cemeteries are on the tour—National, City, and Mt. Olivet—each worth your time to explore (each features a separate map). Some sites are suitable solely for drive-bys as you read the information in the book. For example, Blockhouse Casino is now the site of the City Reservoir, which is closed to the public for security reasons. Some urbanized sites, such as Peach Orchard Hill, may require some imagination on your part.

Historic Preservation

In 2003, the Civil War Preservation Trust listed Nashville as one of the Top Ten Endangered Battlefields in the nation. Significantly, the city government committed $2 million to develop long-neglected Fort Negley into a heritage tourism site. The Battle of Nashville Preservation Society has helped save property at Shy's Hill, Redoubt No. 1, and Kelley's Point. The Sons of Confederate Veterans helped save Granbury's Lunette. Non-profit organizations maintain three antebellum house museums—Travellers Rest, Belmont Mansion, and Belle Meade Plantation. Three major historic cemeteries honor those whose fought on both sides. Churches which served as military hospitals have been preserved by their congregations. The majestic and unique State Capitol still houses the State Assembly and looks much as it did 150 years ago. Recently, the Battle of Nashville Monument was refurbished and relocated to a new park site. Much has been accomplished in recent years, but there is still much to be done. Please support local organizations dedicated to preserving the history of the United States of America.

Civil War Nashville Timeline

1861

Feb. 9	Tennesseans vote against convention to consider secession.
April 13	Fort Sumter.
April 17	Gov. Harris refuses Lincoln's call for military volunteers.
May 2	1st Tennessee Infantry formed in Nashville by Col. George Maney.
June 8	State votes 2-to-1 to declare independence from the Union.

1862

Feb. 6	Fort Henry on Tennessee River captured by U.S. gunboats.
Feb. 16	Fort Donelson on the Cumberland River surrenders to U.S. Grant.
Feb. 23	Confederate army evacuates Nashville.
Feb. 25	Buell's Union troops occupy Nashville.
March 12	Military Governor Andrew Johnson arrives in Nashville.
April 6-7	Battle of Shiloh. Casualties transported to Nashville.
July 13	Cavalry under Forrest raids, captures Murfreesboro.
Aug. 12	Morgan destroys South Tunnel on L&N Railroad near Gallatin.
Nov. 4	Forrest threatens Nashville; Morgan raids Edgefield.
Dec. 26	Rosecrans moves out of Nashville towards Bragg at Murfreesboro.
Dec. 31	Battle of Stones River (Murfreesboro) begins.

1863

Jan. 2	Battle of Stones River concludes; Confederates retreat next day.
June 23	Rosecrans begins Tullahoma Campaign toward Chattanooga.
Nov. 27	Pvt. Sam Davis hanged by Union troops as spy at Pulaski.

1864

Jan. 21	Unionist meeting in Nashville calls for Constitutional Convention.
Nov. 4	Forrest destroys Union river depot at Johnsonville.
Nov. 8	Johnson elected Vice President as Lincoln's running mate.
Nov. 30	Battle of Franklin. Schofield retreats to Nashville.
Dec. 2	Hood's Confederate army takes positions south of Nashville.
Dec. 2-14	CSA cavalry battles Union gunboats on Cumberland near Nashville.
Dec. 5-7	Battle of the Cedars at Murfreesboro.
Dec. 15-16	Battle of Nashville. Hood's army routed by Thomas' Union attack.

1865

Jan. 9	Union delegates hold Constitutional Convention at Capitol.
March 4	Brownlow elected civilian Governor in Unionist election.
April 9	Lee surrenders to Grant at Appomattox.
April 14	Johnson becomes U.S. President after Lincoln assassinated.
April 26	Army of Tennessee surrenders in North Carolina.

1866

July 24	Tennessee readmitted into the Union.

Military Operations in Middle Tennessee, 1862-64

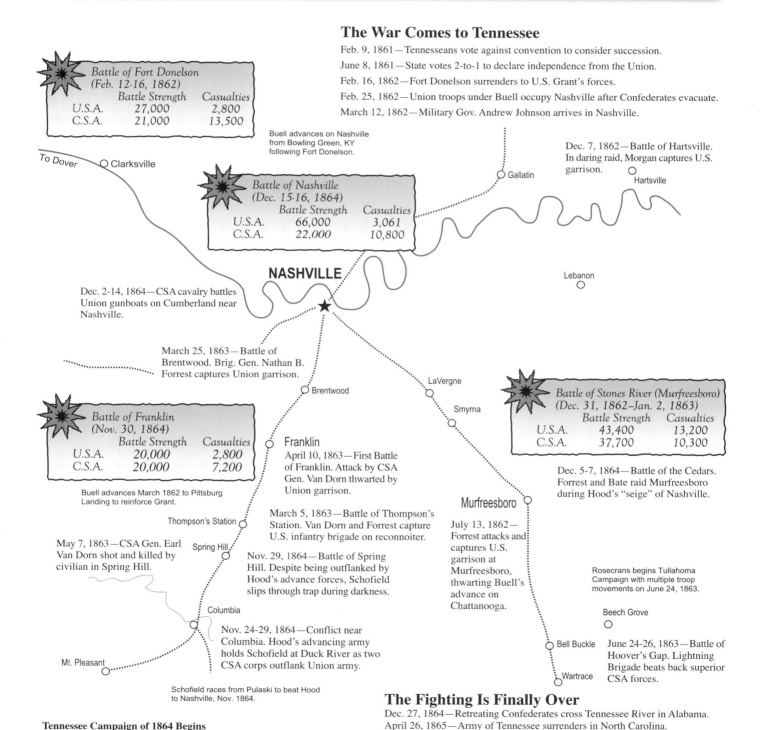

The War Comes to Tennessee

Feb. 9, 1861—Tennesseans vote against convention to consider succession.

June 8, 1861—State votes 2-to-1 to declare independence from the Union.

Feb. 16, 1862—Fort Donelson surrenders to U.S. Grant's forces.

Feb. 25, 1862—Union troops under Buell occupy Nashville after Confederates evacuate.

March 12, 1862—Military Gov. Andrew Johnson arrives in Nashville.

Battle of Fort Donelson
(Feb. 12-16, 1862)

	Battle Strength	Casualties
U.S.A.	27,000	2,800
C.S.A.	21,000	13,500

Buell advances on Nashville from Bowling Green, KY following Fort Donelson.

To Dover ○ Clarksville

Dec. 7, 1862—Battle of Hartsville. In daring raid, Morgan captures U.S. garrison.

○ Gallatin

○ Hartsville

Battle of Nashville
(Dec. 15-16, 1864)

	Battle Strength	Casualties
U.S.A.	66,000	3,061
C.S.A.	22,000	10,800

NASHVILLE

○ Lebanon

Dec. 2-14, 1864—CSA cavalry battles Union gunboats on Cumberland near Nashville.

March 25, 1863—Battle of Brentwood. Brig. Gen. Nathan B. Forrest captures Union garrison.

○ Brentwood

LaVergne ○

Smyrna ○

Battle of Stones River (Murfreesboro)
(Dec. 31, 1862–Jan. 2, 1863)

	Battle Strength	Casualties
U.S.A.	43,400	13,200
C.S.A.	37,700	10,300

Battle of Franklin
(Nov. 30, 1864)

	Battle Strength	Casualties
U.S.A.	20,000	2,800
C.S.A.	20,000	7,200

Buell advances March 1862 to Pittsburg Landing to reinforce Grant.

Franklin

April 10, 1863—First Battle of Franklin. Attack by CSA Gen. Van Dorn thwarted by Union garrison.

March 5, 1863—Battle of Thompson's Station. Van Dorn and Forrest capture U.S. infantry brigade on reconnoiter.

Dec. 5-7, 1864—Battle of the Cedars. Forrest and Bate raid Murfreesboro during Hood's "seige" of Nashville.

Murfreesboro ○

Thompson's Station ○

May 7, 1863—CSA Gen. Earl Van Dorn shot and killed by civilian in Spring Hill.

Spring Hill ○

Nov. 29, 1864—Battle of Spring Hill. Despite being outflanked by Hood's advance forces, Schofield slips through trap during darkness.

July 13, 1862—Forrest attacks and captures U.S. garrison at Murfreesboro, thwarting Buell's advance on Chattanooga.

Rosecrans begins Tullahoma Campaign with multiple troop movements on June 24, 1863.

Columbia ○

Beech Grove ○

Nov. 24-29, 1864—Conflict near Columbia. Hood's advancing army holds Schofield at Duck River as two CSA corps outflank Union army.

Mt. Pleasant ○

Bell Buckle ○

June 24-26, 1863—Battle of Hoover's Gap. Lightning Brigade beats back superior CSA forces.

Wartrace ○

Schofield races from Pulaski to beat Hood to Nashville, Nov. 1864.

The Fighting Is Finally Over

Dec. 27, 1864—Retreating Confederates cross Tennessee River in Alabama.

April 26, 1865—Army of Tennessee surrenders in North Carolina.

July 24, 1866—Tennessee readmitted into the Union.

Tennessee Campaign of 1864 Begins

Nov. 22, 1864—Hood's army marches northward into Tennessee.

The region northwest of Nashville was home to many ironworks, such as the Great Western stack furnace above, found at TVA's Land Between the Lakes Recreation Area north of Dover.

The fall of Fort Henry on the Tennessee River and Fort Donelson on the Cumberland River downstream from Nashville in February 1862 was the key to the invasion of Tennessee by Union gunboats under Flag Officer Andrew Foote and infantry under Brig. Gen. Ulysses S. Grant.

On Feb. 6, Fort Henry was captured relatively quickly due to its poor location on the river. Gunboats of the Union "brown water navy" approached point-blank and fired. Most of the defenders fled eastward to Fort Donelson, although Confederate Gen. Lloyd Tilghman was captured.

Fort Donelson was much more formidable than Fort Henry, boasting a dozen heavy artillery pieces on high ground over the river. On Feb. 14, gunners in the fort exchanged "iron Valentines" with Union gunboats and drove the ironclads away. By this time, however, the outerworks of the fort were nearly surrounded by Grant's infantry units. On Feb. 15, the Confederates massed on their left flank and attempted a breakout toward Nashville. The attack appeared to be successful at first, but confusion in the high command forced the soldiers to retreat back into the fort.

The fort's commander, Gen. John B. Floyd, saw the situation as hopeless and, fearing for his life if captured, turned over command to Brig. Gen. Gideon Pillow and escaped on a steamboat. Pillow followed suit and demurred to Brig. Gen. Simon Buckner. It was Buckner on Feb. 16 who surrendered the fort to former West Point classmate Grant, who became famous not only for the victory but for his words: "No terms except an unconditional and immediate surrender can be accepted."

A little-known cavalry commander, Col. Nathan Bedford Forrest, refused to surrender and led his troops across swollen, icy creeks to safety in Nashville.

Approximately 13,000 Confederate soldiers were taken prisoner and shipped northward to poorly prepared POW camps. The fall of Fort Donelson provoked the "Great Panic" in Nashville, which would also soon fall to Union troops. Along the river route from Dover to Nashville, the Federals occupied Fort Defiance in Clarksville which, contrary to its name, had been abandoned by the Confederates.

Today, the site of Fort Henry lies beneath the waters of Kentucky Lake, although hikers on local trails can still see remains of the outer works (rifle pits).

Fort Donelson National Battlefield preserves the 15-acre earthern fort and its riverside gun batteries. A self-guided tour features eleven sites, including the National Cemetery and the Dover Hotel, also known as Surrender House. The phone number for Fort Donelson National Battlefield is (931) 232-5706. Dover can be reached from Nashville on I-24 and Hwy. 79.

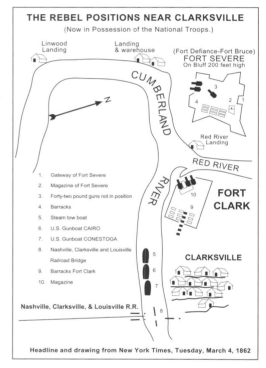

THE REBEL POSITIONS NEAR CLARKSVILLE
(Now in Possession of the National Troops.)

Linwood Landing
Landing & warehouse
(Fort Defiance-Fort Bruce)
FORT SEVERE
On Bluff 200 feet high

CUMBERLAND RIVER
RED RIVER
Red River Landing

FORT CLARK

CLARKSVILLE

1. Gateway of Fort Severe
2. Magazine of Fort Severe
3. Forty-two pound guns not in position
4. Barracks
5. Steam tow boat
6. U.S. Gunboat CAIRO
7. U.S. Gunboat CONESTOGA
8. Nashville, Clarksville and Louisville Railroad Bridge
9. Barracks Fort Clark
10. Magazine

Nashville, Clarksville, & Louisville R.R.

Headline and drawing from New York Times, Tuesday, March 4, 1862

Gen. Simon B. Buckner surrendered Fort Donelson to Gen. U.S. Grant at the old Dover Hotel (Surrender House) on the bank of the Cumberland River. The site is opened to the public during the summer season.

The Surrender of Nashville:

"A Perfect Panic"

During the Great Panic, Confederate currency became nearly worthless. Twenty-dollar bills (this one issued in 1864) bore the likeness of the magnificent Tennessee State Capitol in Nashville.

Church services were suspended the morning of Sunday, Feb. 16, 1862 when news of the surrender of Fort Donelson arrived in Nashville. Unsure what to do, and certain that the dreaded Union gunboats would reduce the city to rubble, the citizens launched into what was described as the "Great Panic."

Depositers rushed the banks, crowds mobbed the warehouses, and southbound trains were filled to overflowing, all while the retreating army of Gen. Albert Sidney Johnston tramped through the city on their journey from Bowling Green, Ky. to Murfreesboro, Tenn. Gen. Johnston subsequently announced that the army would not defend the city.

Mayor R.B. Cheatham, after consulting with Johnston, addressed a crowd at the courthouse, begging for calm and asking his citizens not to burn the city. He said he would surrender the city to Gen. Don Carlos Buell when he arrived. The First Missouri Regiment was assigned to guard the city against harm.

"A perfect panic reigned throughout the whole city," said a local Union loyalist. "The streets were thronged with people wild with excitement."

Gov. Isham Harris, an ardent secessionist, and the state legislature left on a train to Memphis. Despite his position as city quartermaster, railroad magnate Vernon K. Stevenson left the city on a special train. Gunners at Fort Zollicoffer on the Cumberland River west of town abandoned the works.

(Courtesy of Tennessee State Library and Archives)
The Brennan Foundry cast cannon tubes for the Confederacy.

Col. Nathan Bedford Forrest arrived from Fort Donelson, and worked to save the city's war munitions. Military goods were produced for the Confederacy in Nashville—cannons, gun carriages, muskets, ball and shot, swords, percussion caps, saddles and harnesses, and gray uniform cloth. Friction primers were produced at the laboratory at the University of Nashville. Overall, there were 73 manufacturers employing 1,318 workers.

Prominent Confederates fled the city. Judge John Overton left his wife Harriet Maxwell Overton to manage their 3500-acre estate, Travellers Rest. Joseph Acklen of Belmont left to tend his extensive cotton plantations in Louisiana, never to return.

Also leaving was John Bell, former Congressman, U.S. senator, and presidential nominee of the Constitutional Union Party in 1860. Methodist ministers, many of whom were the most vocal advocates of the Confederacy, left town, some to minister to the Army of Tennessee. Sarah Childress Polk, widow of President James K. Polk, remained in Nashville and stayed at Polk Place the remainder of the war.

Wounded Union prisoners of war arrived by steamboat from Fort Donelson and were housed at the incompleted Maxwell House Hotel, now called the Zollicoffer Barracks.

On Tues., Feb. 18, mobs broke into government warehouses, and Col. Forrest and his cavalrymen were forced to charge the mob before it would disperse. Several days later, the mobs returned and Forrest countered by turning the city's fire-engine hose on them.

On Wednesday, trains continued to ship supplies out of town during thunderstorms and torrential rains. That night the floor of the 700-foot-long suspension bridge was set ablaze and then the cables were cut. After midnight the railroad bridge, with the longest draw in the nation, was set afire and completely destroyed.

On Sun., Feb. 23, the Union advance guard reached the small city of Edgefield, directly across the Cumberland River from Nashville. The next day, Union Gen. Don Carlos Buell reached Edgefield from Bowling Green.

On Tues., Feb. 25, the gunboat *U.S.S. Cairo* led a flotilla of seven troop transports into Nashville, bringing 10,000 troops under Gen. William "Bull" Nelson. The 6th Ohio Volunteer Infantry disembarked and proceeded up Cedar Street to the State Capitol. At 8:45 a.m., Gen. Nelson hoisted the regimental flag of the 6th Ohio over the Capitol. Then the American flag of former New England ship captain William Driver was hoisted over the east entrance. Driver, who had retired to Nashville, was a well-known local Union loyalist who had hid his ship's flag from the Confederates inside a bed comforter. He had called his cherished American flag "Old Glory," and from then on the U.S. flag has been known as Old Glory.

Mayor Cheatham and ten citizens crossed the river by steamer to Edgefield and officially surrendered the city to Gen. Buell. The bands of the 36th Indiana and the 24th, 41st, and 51st Ohio regiments entertained a curious crowd by playing Dixie.

A Northern newspaper correspondent stated that "there is but little Union sentiment expressed here, in fact, far less than I had anticipated. All hands appear to hate us cordially."

On March 1, Gen. Buell moved into the St. Cloud Hotel. He paid his respects to Mrs. Polk, a precedent followed by all succeeding Federal commanders. Later, Buell selected the house of George W. Cunningham at 13 North High St. as his residence, two blocks south of the Capitol.

On March 3, President Lincoln appointed Sen. Andrew Johnson of Greeneville, Tenn. to be military governor of Tennessee, a position he would hold for the next 34 months. Late in the night of March 12 Johnson entered Nashville "without display" and checked into the St. Cloud Hotel.

Gunboats and Transports
Cumberland River provided route of invasion, supply line

The Cumberland River played an important role in Nashville history during the Civil War, just as it had Christmas Day 1799, when settlers from North Carolina walked across the frozen river and established Fort Nashborough on the bluffs overlooking the ice. Since then, the river, which flows northward to the Ohio, has been the city's main water thoroughfare.

The fall of Nashville to U.S. troops was precipitated by the Union capture of Fort Donelson downstream on the Cumberland. Confederate Fort Defiance in Clarksville and Fort Zollicoffer near Nashville never saw action, abandoned by their crews before the boats arrived. The U.S. troops which first occupied Nashville arrived on steam transports, escorted by ironclad gunboats.

At that time, there were two bridges across the river, linking Nashville with the small town of Edgefield. The evening of Wed., Feb. 19, the 700-foot-long suspension bridge over the Cumberland was set ablaze by the Confederates and the cables were cut. At the same time, the wooden platform of the railroad bridge, a swing-span structure, was set ablaze. The two burning bridges produced a "strikingly beautiful scene," according to one spectator. Two nights before, the Confederates had burned two steamboats tied at the Broad Street landing near the main wharf. Many in the city at first feared it was the soldiers burning the city before it fell into enemy hands.

On Feb. 25, the mayor took a steamer across the river to Edgefield to surrender the city to the Union troops.

By March 24, 1862, there were 110 steamboats on the Cumberland River hauling provisions to Nashville.

"The street next to the river is piled with accoutrements of the army, with guns, wagons, ammunition, etc., at the extent of which the rebels stare in astonishment," wrote a correspondent of a Columbus, Ohio newspaper.

Major Gen. Henry Halleck reinstated the right of Nashvillians to trade with Northern states in order to put steamboats on the Cumberland to transport troops without disclosing that purpose.

By May, permits had been issued to ship 3,000 bales of cotton to the North.

On June 11, 1862, the railroad bridge over the Cumberland had been rebuilt and opened for use again. It was fortified against attackers.

A pontoon bridge was built across the river by using ice barges to support a roadway for wagons and pedestrians. The bridge rose and fell with the river.

By mid-1863 Nashville was the supply center

U.S.S. Cairo

Ironclad gunboats ruled the riverways

One of the most feared weapons of the Union invasion was the ironclad gunboat. The gunboats, in joint operations with the U.S. Army, defeated the Confederate river defenses, escorted convoys of supply-laden steam transports, and prowled the Cumberland River for bands of partisans and guerillas.

The first convoy of transports filled with blueclad soldiers which reached Nashville on Feb. 25, 1862 was led by the *U.S.S. Cairo,* one of the seven custom-built ironclad gunboats (City Class) named after cities along the upper Mississippi and Ohio rivers. The others were *Carondelet, Cincinnati, Louisville, Mound City, Pittsburg* and *St. Louis.*

The City Class ironclads were identified by colored bands on the smokestacks. The ironclads were known as "Pook's turtles," after Samuel Pook, who designed the boats to be massive, flat-bottomed paddlewheelers which could cruise upstream on the narrow rivers, drawing only six feet of water.

The boats were built under contract by river engineer James B. Eads at Mound City, Ill. and commissioned on Jan. 15, 1862. (Eads later built the first bridge over the Mississippi River at St. Louis.)

The gunboat's above-water structure was sloped at 35 degrees to deflect cannon shells and was constructed of 2.5 inches of charcoal plate iron backed by two feet of white oak timbers.

The vessel's five fire-tube boilers operated at 140 psi steam pressure and consumed nearly a ton of coal per hour. The ironclad could make way at six knots.

Each ironclad was armed with 13 big guns—four on each side, three in the bow, and two in the stern. These consisted of:
- Three 42-pound army rifles
- Three 64-pound navy smoothbores
- Six 32-pound navy smoothbores
- One 32-pound Parrott gun

The *U.S.S. Cairo* was manned by 17 officers and 158 enlisted men. The captain was Lt. Commander Thomas O. Selfridge, Jr.

On Dec. 12, 1862 on the Yazoo River in Mississippi, the *U.S.S. Cairo* became the first ship to be sunk by an electrically detonated torpedo (mine).

The sunken ship was discovered in 1956, and the pilothouse, cannon, and other artifacts were recovered in 1960. Much, but not all, of the structure was raised in 1964, and the restored ship was put on permanent display in 1977 at Vicksburg National Military Park, where it can be seen today.

for armies in the Western Theater. Supplies manufactured or warehoused in Louisville and Cincinnati were transported down the Ohio to the Cumberland River at Smithland, Ky., then upstream to Nashville.

During March 1864, 213 steamboats delivered and unloaded 62,666 tons of cargo at the city's two river levies. A third levy was added. During the summer and early fall of 1864 the quarter-master's corps handled 2,000 tons of supplies each day for a period of 150 consecutive days.

In May 1864, the Nashville & Northwestern Railroad opened all the way westward to the Tennessee River, where a huge Union supply depot was built at Johnsonville.

The new rail line of supply had been necessitated by two factors affecting the river—seasonal low water levels which prohibited the passage of large river vessels and the attacks by Confederate cavalry and partisan guerillas.

Detail of naval gun.

There wasn't much that could be done about the low water, but the Federals did take action against guerilla activity.

On Jan. 13, 1863, Gen. Joseph Wheeler's Confederate cavalry seized three steamboats bound for Louisville with wounded soldiers. All of the wounded were placed on one ship and the other two were burned, as was a responding gunboat.

On the same day, irregulars led by Capt. Dick McCann brought to, boarded, and burned a Nashville-bound transport loaded with hay and corn.

At first, Union commanding Gen. William Rosecrans had trouble coordinating with the naval commanders, including Lt. Commander Leroy Fitch. After Secretary of War Edwin Stanton and General-in-Chief Henry Halleck intervened on Rosecrans' behalf, there were six gunboats patrolling the Cumberland—the *Lexington, Fairplay, Brilliant, Saint Clair, Silver Lake,* and *Robb.*

Fitch ordered the gunboats to "fire at any person seen loafing through the woods or standing on the banks at suspicious places or near where boats had been molested."

On Jan. 29, 1863, four Union gunboats escorted 31 steamboats and additional river barges into Nashville after the *U.S.S. Lexington* had raided and burned a warehouse used by the Confederates 20 miles above Clarksville.

Several days later, Wheeler and Gen. Nathan Bedford Forrest raided the Union garrison at Fort Donelson and were thwarted by the arrival of six Union gunboats which had been escorting a convoy.

River vessels also were deployed from Nashville to handle military matters upstream on the Cumberland.

In the fall of 1863, the Union garrison at Knoxville, commanded by Gen. Ambrose Burnside, needed supplies and food. On Nov. 13, river transports left Nashville and traveled to the river town of Carthage with 300,000 rations of salt meat and one million rations of all other kinds. The ships were escorted by two gunboats, *Reindeer* and *Silver Lake.*

The day after Christmas 1863 a steamboat expedition left Nashville for the upper Cumberland with 143 sharpshooters of the 70th Indiana Infantry and the 129th Illinois. The three

transports were escorted by the *Reindeer* and the *Silver Lake II.* They destroyed flatboats near Gainesboro and verified the presence of guerillas upstream in Jackson County.

The route from the Ohio River to Nashville was fraught with danger. In late July 1863, the steamboat *St. Louis,* enroute from Louisville, was seized and burned by raiders 20 miles below Clarksville. By December of 1863, no private boats were allowed to enter the Cumberland River at Smithland unless they were under government charter or carrying government freight.

After Brig. Gen. James L. Donaldson became Quartermaster in Nashville in February 1864, the U.S. Army stopped leasing steamboats by the day and purchased them outright. He also stopped chartering boats by the day for transporting supplies from the North to Nashville and contracted for freight charges by the hundred-weight, which was cheaper.

In the summer of 1864 the nine-acre United States Shipyard was built on the Edgefield side of the river north of the railroad bridge to build and repair river boats and barges. By August 20 the shipyard had overhauled the steamboat *Mattie Cobler,* nearly completed work on new ferryboat, and just received for repairs the ram *M.V. Baird.* The first barge built there, the *Kearsarge,* was launched Oct. 17.

Confederate Gen. Hood's advance to Nashville in late 1864 increased military activity on the river. Lt. Commander Fitch was in Nashville with two ironclads and other gunboats to make regular patrols above and below Nashville by late November.

At dusk on Dec. 1, steamboats brought the first 5,000 men of Gen. Andrew J. Smith's three divisions from St. Louis to help defend Nashville against Hood's Army of Tennessee. The remaining 9,000 men from the Missouri-Kansas frontier arrived just before midnight. One of their transports, the *W.L. Ewing,* had hit a snag below St. Louis and sank with no fatalities.

On Dec. 6, in a famous cavalry-naval battle, Fitch's U.S. gunboat escort was driven back at Bell's Bend, nine miles downstream from Nashville. Even if the boats had gotten through, they probably would have been trapped by low water on the Cumberland near the Harpeth Shoals.

River traffic on the Cumberland had come to a standstill. The railroad to the north was Nashville's only lifeline. Gen. Hood's men arrived at Nashville on Dec. 2. The Union hospital ship *D.A. January* waited at the wharf for patients.

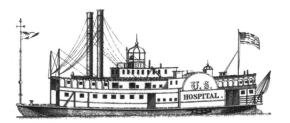

Union hospital ship D.A. January
(Military Atlas of the Civil War)

Beans and Bullets
U.S. Military Railroads supplied advancing Union armies

If the initial invasion of the South was led by gunboats plying the rivers, it was the railroad that sustained the territorial gains of the U.S. Army and provided the main mode of transportation.

At the time of occupation, Nashville was served by five railroad companies:

- Louisville & Nashville R.R.—The main line of supply between Nashville and the North. The station in Nashville was the city's largest and busiest. Two vital sections were the bridge over the Cumberland at Nashville and the South Tunnel near Gallatin in Sumner County.
- Nashville & Clarksville R.R.: Known antebellum as the Edgefield & Kentucky. This short line linked Nashville at the Edgefield Junction with Clarksville via a connection to the Memphis, Clarksville & Louisville at the Kentucky state line.
- Nashville & Chattanooga R.R.—Main line of supply for the Union advances against Chattanooga and Atlanta. The railway ran southeasterly to Stevenson, Ala., where it joined the Memphis & Charleston and ran east to Chattanooga, a total of 151 miles. The tunnel at Cowan was 2,228 feet long, bored through Cumberland Mountain in 1849-53 by crews of English and Irish immigrants and black slaves using only black-powder blasting and hand tools.
- Nashville & Decatur R.R.—Also known as the Tennessee & Alabama. This line ran due south 119 miles to Decatur, Ala., where it connected with the Memphis & Charleston.
- Nashville & Northwestern R.R.—Incomplete and running only 28 miles to Kingston Springs at the beginning of the war, this railway in 1864 was extended the full 78 miles westward to the Tennessee River, where Union forces built a huge supply depot.

Federal forces were authorized by an Act of Congress (Jan. 31, 1862) to seize any railroad necessary to support military operations. Eventually, all railroads in and out of Nashville were commandeered by the U.S. military for their exclusive use.

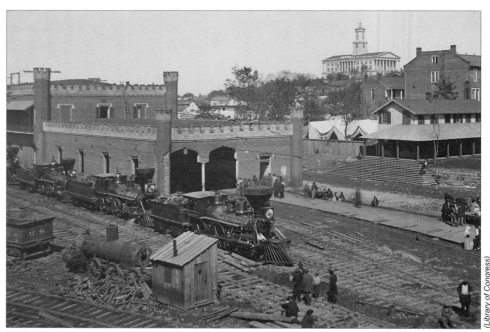

(Library of Congress)

The Nashville & Chattanooga railyard in Nashville, west of the State Capitol (visible in upper right).

The first railroad locomotive, Tennessee No. 1, was delivered to Nashville on Dec. 13, 1850 on the steamboat *Beauty* from Cincinnati. Teams of mules were used to haul the steam engine one mile on improvised tracks from the wharf to South Cherry Street. A trial run of one mile was made from that point on Dec. 27. A historical marker can be viewed on 4th Ave. South and Hart Street, just south of the City Cemetery.

Nearly 1,200 miles of railway were built in Tennessee during the decade of the 1850s.

Supplying the armies

Massive quantities of war material, foodstuffs, and forage passed through Nashville on the railroads as the Union armies moved farther south. Supplies came from Louisville over the rails or on steam transports and barges moving downstream on the Ohio River and then upstream on the Cumberland to the Nashville wharf or upstream on the Tennessee River to the depot at Johnsonville.

By mid-1863, Nashville was the supply center for all of the armies in the Western Theater.

When named by the War Department as general manager of all the railroads in the Nashville sector, L&N R.R. engineer John B. Anderson promised Gen. Grant that he would send 80 to 100 carloads of supplies to Chattanooga each day.

During the 1864 Atlanta campaign, Gen. William T. Sherman's armies constituted 98,000 men and 35,000 horses and mules. Supplies were needed 20 days ahead of requirements.

From November 1863 through August 1864, the following supplies passed through Nashville headed to the Atlanta campaign:

- 41,122 horses and 38,724 mules
- 3,795 wagons
- 445,355 pairs of shoes
- 290,000 blankets
- 529,000 tents
- millions of bushels of corn and oats, and tens of thousands of tons of hay

Gen. Robert Allen, chief quartermaster in the Western Theater said, "No army in the world was ever better provided than Sherman's."

Often the rails became doubly important as low water on the Cumberland River would temporarily prevent steam transports from reaching Nashville.

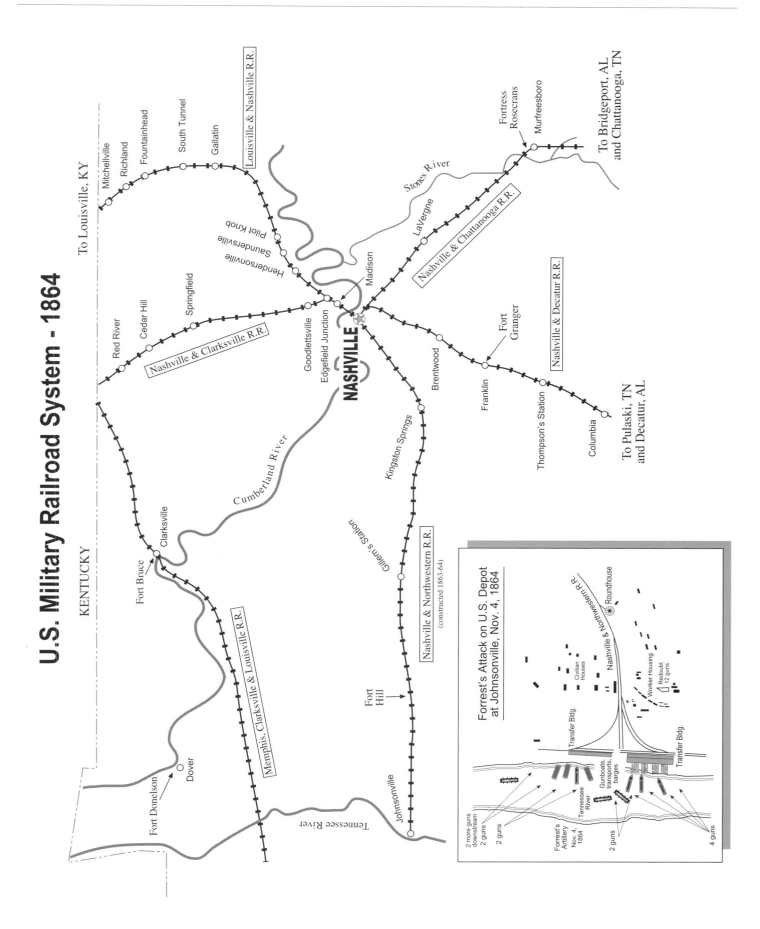

U.S. Military Railroad System - 1864

To Louisville, KY

KENTUCKY

Mitchellville
Richland
Fountainhead
South Tunnel
Gallatin

Louisville & Nashville R.R.

Pilot Knob
Saundersville
Hendersonville

Stones River

Fortress Rosecrans
Murfreesboro

To Bridgeport, AL and Chattanooga, TN

LaVergne

Nashville & Chattanooga R.R.

Madison

Red River
Cedar Hill
Springfield

Goodlettsville
Edgefield Junction

NASHVILLE

Nashville & Clarksville R.R.

Brentwood

Fort Granger

Franklin

Thompson's Station

Nashville & Decatur R.R.

Columbia

To Pulaski, TN and Decatur, AL

Cumberland River

Kingston Springs

Clarksville

Fort Bruce

Fort Donelson

Dover

Memphis, Clarksville & Louisville R.R.

Gillem's Station

Fort Hill

Nashville & Northwestern R.R.
(constructed 1863-64)

Johnsonville

Tennessee River

Forrest's Attack on U.S. Depot at Johnsonville, Nov. 4, 1864

Nashville & Northwestern R.R.
Roundhouse

Civilian Houses

Worker Housing

Redoubt 12 guns

Transfer Bldg.

Transfer Bldg.

Gunboats, transports, barges

Tennessee River

2 more guns downstream
2 guns
2 guns

Forrest's Artillery Nov. 4, 1864

2 guns

4 guns

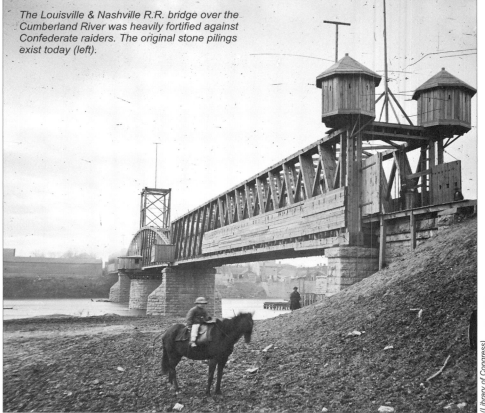

The Louisville & Nashville R.R. bridge over the Cumberland River was heavily fortified against Confederate raiders. The original stone pilings exist today (left).

(Library of Congress)

Sometimes the heavy use of the railroads by the military resulted in deprivations on the part of civilians. In February 1863, 60 carloads of freight accumulated at Louisville waiting for clearance. The supply of coal was exhausted by the Nashville Gas Light Co. and the lights went out, including those used by the Union military. Consequently, river barges of coal were brought in with the help of the local military.

Nashville facilities expanded

The Federals greatly expanded the rail facilities in Nashville, building a new roundhouse and maintenance shops near the main N&C R.R. terminal in the "gulch" west of the State Capitol. The coal yard could hold four million bushels.

In charge of processing all of the material moving through Nashville was Quartermaster and Brig. Gen. James L. Donaldson, who directed the construction of three huge warehouses:
• The Taylor Depot at the Broad Street terminus of the Nashville & Decatur R.R. covered two-thirds of the area from Broad to Demonbreun and extended west to the railroad. Fifty wagons could be loaded or unloaded at one time.
• The Eaton Depot, for subsistence stores, located just south of the Taylor Depot on the same railroad.
• A grain storage depot at the Nashville & Northwestern R.R.

In February 1864 a few hundred yards of track were laid from the upper wharf on the Cumberland River to the Nashville & Chattanooga depot, to facilitate shipments from steamboat to southbound rail cars. Coach service was supplied by J. Lee Able

"Whoever cannot give a good account of themselves, shoot or hang in the nearest tree." Instructions to U.S. railroad guards from commanding Gen. William Rosecrans.

between the wharves and rail depots.

By the spring of 1864, the principal shops of the United States Military Railroads, Division of the Mississippi, had been consolidated at Nashville. Maintenance was performed on all 221 locomotives of the division as well as rail cars.

It is estimated that there were 30,000 U.S. government civilian employees in Nashville working for the quartermaster or in the railroad shops. Most of them had been recruited up North. One fourth brought their families with them. And most moved back North after the war was over, but not all.

Soldiers, the wounded, prisoners

Troops themselves were often quickly transported from one area of operations to another. After major battles, the wounded and the dead flowed into the city, as well as prisoners of war on their way to Northern prison camps.

In the first ten months of 1864, 140,000 Federal troops were transported south from Nashville and 40,000 sick and wounded

and 50,000 volunteers were returned from the front.

The railways were overflowing with wounded soldiers following the major battles of Shiloh in April 1862, Stones River in January 1863, Chickamauga in September 1863, the battles for Atlanta in May-Sept. 1864, and Franklin in November 1864.

On July 26, 1864, the body of Union Major Gen. James B. McPherson, killed at the Battle of Atlanta, arrived at the Nashville & Chattanooga depot. The train was met by a delegation of 100 ranking officers, including generals Andrew Johnson, Alvan Gillem, Joseph D. Webster, Robert H. Milroy and Augustus L. Chetlain.

A solemn procession escorted the body to the Louisville depot, including an artillery battery and two regiments and their bands.

From November 1863 through August 1864, 10,000 Confederate prisoners of war were transported from the front to Northern POW camps. On July 10-11, 1864, a total of 1,333 prisoners arrived from nothern Georgia. It was not uncommon for citizens to witness Confederate prisoners marched through the streets of the city.

Railroads fortified against attack

Constant traffic on the railways was vital to the Union war effort as Federal armies advanced toward Chattanooga and Atlanta. The Confederates, of course, knew this and repeatedly attacked trains and the rails, especially at bridges and trestles. The Federals were forced to build fortifications at these vital points and provide soldiers to guard against enemy attacks.

The main bridge at Nashville over the Cumberland was an impressive feat of engineering, built in the 1850s in a swing-span design with massive stone piers (which can been seen today). The center span could pivot to allow passage of steamboats with tall smokestacks. It had the longest draw of any railroad bridge at that time. On Feb. 19, 1862, the retreating Confederates burned the wooden platform of the bridge. It was rebuilt by the occupying Federals and opened again to trains on June 11. Gen. John Carlos Buell ordered a stockade built on the Edgefield side of the river and that the bridge be fortified. Guard turrets were built at both ends of the bridge and the trestlework was planked, with loopholes allowing infantry on the bridge to fire at attackers.

After the Battle of Stones River, Union troops constructed a supply depot just northwest of Murfreesboro and named it Fortress Rosecrans. The 200-acre fort, the largest earthen fortification built during the war, could hold enough supplies to feed 50,000 troops for up to 90 days. Redoubts guarded the Nashville & Chattanooga railroad and the Nashville Turnpike, both of which ran through the fortifications. (See page 71 for more information.)

Seven blockhouses were built between Nashville and Murfreesboro to protect bridges across the streams. All except the one at Overall Creek near the fort were burned by the Confederates during Hood's 1864 campaign.

In all, the Union built 47 blockhouses on the Nashville & Chattanooga between those two cities to protect bridges and trestles. Such structures were built of wood and were extremely vulnerable.

Fort Granger was built in Franklin to protect the Nashville & Decatur crossing at the Harpeth River. (See page 72 for more information.)

> *Upon inspection, blockhouses were sometimes found abandoned, the troops out in the woods cutting firewood for pay for government contractors. Several officers were court-martialed and the practice ceased.*

A typical railroad blockhouse used to protect bridges and trestles. (Library of Congress)

> *Orders were issued by the U.S. military prohibiting the men from bathing in the railroad water towers because the soapy water would foam up in the locomotive boilers.*

Confederate cavalry raids

The railroads were attacked often by Confederate cavalry under the commands of Gen. John Hunt Morgan, Gen. Nathan Bedford Forrest, and Gen. Joseph Wheeler. In addition, smaller bands of partisans and guerillas played havoc with the smooth operation of the railways. The most notable of these were Major Dick McCann and Capt. Duval McNairy.

In August 1862, Morgan successfully attacked the stockades at Pilot Knob, Saundersville, Drakes Creek, and Manskers Creek along the Louisville & Nashville R.R. and took 163 prisoners. The 20 Union infantrymen stationed at the Edgefield Junction stockade, however, repulsed three attacks over three hours and inflicted 26 casualties.

Five days after the Battle of Stones River, McCann led irregulars on a raid that destroyed a locomotive and construction train on the Nashville & Chattanooga and captured the crew and guards. In retribution, the Nashville post commander, Gen. Mitchell, ordered the 85th Illinois Infantry Regiment to burn all the houses and barns owned by McCann and his associate, Thomas Chilcut.

On April 10, 1863, Gen. Wheeler attacked a Louisville & Nashville R.R. train nine miles northeast of Nashville with an artillery ambush from across the Cumberland River at 500-yard range. Twenty-one rounds destroyed the locomotive and killed most of the cargo in the 18 rail cars—horses and livestock. Wheeler also ambushed another train at Antioch south of Nashville and captured 20 Federal officers and a large

quantity of mail.

On Sept. 1, 1863, Capt. McNairy, a Nashville Confederate cavalryman who organized and commanded partisan units behind the lines, lead a raid on the Nashville & Northwestern R.R., burning fuel wood and capturing black laborers.

In the late summer of 1864, Wheeler's men attacked Sherman's supply lines, cutting telegraph lines, burning crossties, and heating and bending rails on the Nashville & Chattanooga R.R.

On Sept. 1, 1864, Gen. Lovell Rousseau moved out of Nashville and confronted Wheeler at Lavergne. Rousseau's men were driven two miles back toward Nashville, and three days later again engaged Wheeler south of Franklin on the Nashville & Decatur R.R., driving the Confederates southward.

Riders encountered dangers

Not all the dangers of railroad transportation were due to fighting. On Sept. 28, 1863, a steam locomotive exploded after leaving the Nashville station bound for Stevenson, Ala. while passing through the Broad Street cut. Fortunately, there were no reported fatalities.

On April 6, 1864, a train enroute to Chattanooga exploded near Murfreesborough. The next day, a train bound for Louisville left the track in Kentucky after encountering a piece of equipment left by a construction crew. Three were killed and 60 injured on a siding near Gallatin in a massive pileup. A southbound locomotive hit a stray horse on a bridge over the Duck River. One man was killed and several injured in an accident on the Nashville & Northwestern near Waverly.

L&N's South Tunnel blocked

One vital railroad structure was the South Tunnel located six miles from Gallatin, north of Nashville on the Louisville & Nashville R.R. On Aug. 12, 1862, Gen. John Hunt Morgan's cavalry captured the Union garrison at Gallatin and then drove a captured locomotive inside the tunnel and burned the inner wooden support structure, blocking 800 feet of the 1000-foot tunnel. The "Thunderbolt of the Confederacy" then burned 40 railroad cars and the bridge at Pilot Knob and retreated to Hartsville.

The quartermaster at Nashville was forced to build a railroad siding and unloading ramp at Mitchellville, 10 miles

Sullivan's Branch No. 2 trestle on the Nashville and Northwestern Railroad in Cheatham County 10 miles west of Bellevue. Pictured is the photographic train of J.F. Coonley, hired by the U.S. Army to photograph all bridges, trestles, and other railroad facilities.

(Courtesy of Tennessee State Library and Archives)

north of the disabled tunnel, and transport supplies the remainder of the way to Nashville in guarded convoys of up to 500 wagons.

Eventually the tunnel was cleared, and passage was reopened to rail traffic on Nov. 26.

Blockage of the tunnel and low water on Cumberland River restricted the flow of supplies during the autumn of 1862, forcing troops to be put on half rations. Soldiers patroled the streets to prevent theft and looting.

The Nashville & Northwestern R.R.

The tunnel blockage was a major factor in the decision to extend the Nashville & Northwestern R.R. from Kingston Springs to the Tennessee River. Supplies coming from Louisville down the Ohio River and up the Tennessee River could then be transported by rail to Nashville.

On Sept. 1, 1863, work commenced on the new section of track. Free blacks and contrabands (runaway slaves) were impressed by the army to build the railroad. Many of these laborers were mustered into the U.S. Colored Troops, 12th and 13th Regiments, who subsequently manned the blockhouses built under the supervision of Capt. W.E. Merrill, Chief Engineer of the Army of the Cumberland, which guarded the many trestles and bridges along the Nashville & Northwestern.

(Library of Congress)

Keeping the railways repaired and running was tedious, hard work but vital to military operations.

On Sept. 27, military governor Andrew Johnson advertised for 1,000 men, white or black, to work on the railroad. Slave owners would be paid $300 for each slave and freedmen would be paid $10 a month. The local newspaper advised the Unionist slave owners to take the offer because the longer they waited the less they would receive for their slaves.

By Oct. 3, however, only 230 blacks had responded to Johnson's call. Additional men were impressed, including 240 refugees.

Missouri engineers came from Corinth, Miss. to help build the new railroad.

By February 1864, crews were laying one-third to three-fourths of a mile of track each day. River barges brought two locomotives and several rail cars for the new line. However, by April 13, a week before the deadline, 25 to 30 miles of track still needed to be built.

On May 19 at 6 a.m., a train of cars pulled out of Nashville and traveled the 78 miles westward to the Tennessee River and returned the same day. Onboard were military governor Johnson, Mayor Smith, and Gens. Granger and Gillem, and Col. Browning.

The Johnsonville Depot

The western terminus of the Nashville & Northwestern R.R. at the river was Johnsonville, a huge Union supply depot. Facilities included a narrow and a wide transfer building with machinery to lift cargo from transports and barges into the warehouses. A redoubt and a blockhouse were built on a hill overlooking the depot. A roundhouse with turntable serviced the freight trains arriving from and departing to Nashville.

The Johnsonville depot was a vital facility in the effort to transport supplies to Gen. Sherman's armies in Georgia. After the surrender of Atlanta, CSA Gen. John Bell Hood turned north in a campaign which would eventually conclude with the Battle of Nashville. As part of the effort

At Johnsonville, supplies were unloaded from river transports and stored in warehouses. The supplies were then loaded onto trains and shipped to Nashville and beyond.

to destroy Sherman's line of supply, Gen. Nathan Bedford Forrest's cavalry, armed with 12 artillery pieces, bombarded the Johnsonville depot on Nov. 4, 1864 from across the Tennessee River. At first, the cannonade struck against the nine Federal gunboats just arrived from Paducah, Ky. Then the artillery took aim at the depot itself. As the warehouses began to burn, the Federals panicked. The commander, Col. C.R. Thompson, ordered the supplies destroyed because he falsely believed that Forrest would cross the river and capture the garrison. Forrest's raid destroyed four gunboats, 14 transports, 17 barges, 33 pieces of artillery, and up to 120,000 tons of quartermaster stores. The total loss was estimated at $2 million to $6 million. Two of Forrest's men were killed and nine wounded. They took 150 prisoners.

Hood's invasion inflicts damage

As Hood approached Franklin and Nashville, people thronged the Nashville & Northwestern R.R. depots, trying to board eastbound trains headed to Nashville. At Johnsonville, the U.S. Colored Troops, including the 2nd U.S. Colored Light Artillery, were ordered to abandon the railroad, destroy surplus weapons, and return to defend Nashville. They arrived in the capital city by Dec. 7, five days after Hood arrived at Nashville.

Two hundred soldiers of the 43rd

The 2nd U.S. Colored Light Artillery Battery prepares to depart Johnsonville for Nashville to meet Hood's Confederate advance in December 1864.

Wisconsin retreated from Johnsonville, marching to the Nashville & Chattanooga depot to sleep on the floor crowded with refugees, awakened at midnight by trains bearing 600 wounded from Franklin.

The damage to the Nashville & Northwestern R.R. was inventoried following the battle at Nashville. Fifteen bridges had

been destroyed and four others partially destroyed. All eleven water tanks along the route were damaged and two completely destroyed. Telegraph lines were cut in 19 places. All government and railroad buildings and warehouses were destroyed save for one blockhouse. One of the four sawmills along the route was destroyed.

Minnesota State Monument

U.S.C.T. Statue

Main Entrance Gate

NASHVILLE NATIONAL CEMETERY

This hallowed ground was established as a U.S. Military Cemetery on Jan. 28, 1867. Originally there were 16,489 burials of known Union soldiers and employees: 38 officers, 10,300 white soldiers, 1,447 colored soldiers, and 703 employees. Among the unknown, there were 3,098 white soldiers, 463 colored soldiers, and 29 employees.

The Union deceased were gathered from an extensive region of Middle Tennessee and southern Kentucky. The number of distinct burial places from which these bodies were taken was 251. A large proportion of the dead, however, were transferred from the hospital burial grounds in and around Nashville and from the nearby battlefields of Franklin and Gallatin, Tenn. Reinterments were also made from Bowling Green and Cave City, Ky.

Key to Numbered Locations on Map on Page 17:

1-Minnesota State Monument (1920). Minnesota lost more soldiers at the Battle of Nashville, Dec. 15-16, 1864, than any other single engagement.

2-Statue of U.S. Colored Troops soldier, dedicated in 2006.

3-Col. Edward S. Jones, Commander, 3rd Penna. Cavalry. Founder and commander of the Tenn.-Ga. Dept. of the Grand Army of the Republic.

4-Col. James W. Lawless, 5th Ky. Cavalry. A native of Ireland, he came to the U.S. at the age of 16.

5-Chaplain Erastus M. Cravath, 101st Ohio Volunteer Infantry Regiment. He was one of the founders of historically black Fisk University in Nashville and served as its president for 25 years.

6-West Patterson, 4th Penna. Volunteer Cavalry. "Teacher of freedmen for 31 years."

7-James A. Leonard, 1st Kansas Battery. His spire is one of oldest in cemetery. He was killed by guerillas in January 1864.

VICINITY MAP

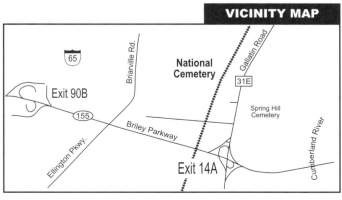

Many U.S. Colored Troops are buried at the National Cemetery.

One of the many gravestones of unidentified U.S. soldiers.

NASHVILLE NATIONAL CEMETERY
1420 Gallatin Road South, Madison, TN
Office: (615) 860-0086
Grave Locator Kiosk at Administration Building

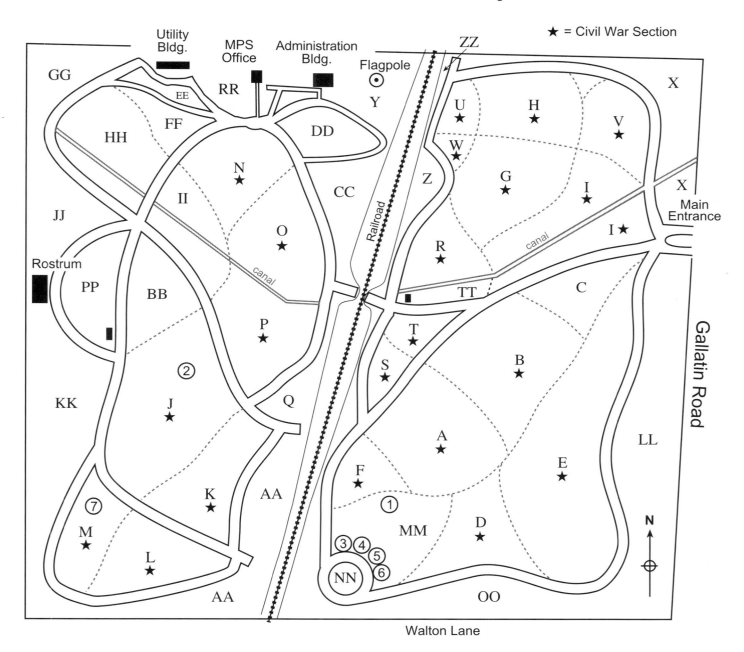

Cemetery open dawn to dusk. Office open M-F, 8-4:30.
Cemetery located six miles north of downtown. Take I-65 North to Briley Parkway East to Gallatin Road North.
Cemetery located just north of intersection on your left.

(2) State Capitol

National Historic Landmark

The Tennessee State Capitol appears today much as it did during the Civil War. Begun in 1845 and completed in 1859, the Capitol was regarded as the most magnificent stone building in the United States outside Washington, D.C. Built on Campbell's Hill (or Cedar Knob), the unique 205-foot-tall tower of the Greek Revival building could be seen for miles in every direction. Today the only view unobstructed by modern skyscrapers is from the north.

During the war, the State Capitol was used by Andrew Johnson, the military governor during the Union occupation. The Capitol was transformed into Fort Andrew Johnson. Earthworks, cotton bales, and palisades with loopholes were constructed around the perimeter of the building, and large, seige-type cannons were stationed at its base, trained on the city below it. The cannons were never fired in anger, only for tributes or demonstrations, but the threat remained. Union troops pitched tents and camped out on Capitol Hill.

The Capitol follows the plan of an Ionic temple, with porticoes on all four facades and a total of 28 Greek columns, four feet in diameter and 33 feet high. The building was designed by noted architect William Strickland, apprentice to the architect of the U.S. Capitol.

Touring Information

The State Capitol is located in downtown Nashville on Charlotte Avenue between 6th and 7th avenues. The Capitol is open Mon.-Fri., 8-4, with free guided tours at 9, 10, and 11 a.m. and at 1, 2, and 3 p.m. Use west entrance across from State Library (handicapped entrance at 6th and Union). Reservations required for groups of ten or more. All adults need photo ID. Cameras are allowed. For information, contact the State Museum at (615) 741-0830.

Military governor ruled state with iron fist

Statue of Andrew Johnson on Capitol grounds

On the night of March 12, 1862, Andrew Johnson, newly appointed by President Lincoln as the military governor of Tennessee, slipped quietly into Nashville. At that time there were about 200 loyal Unionists in the city.

The next evening he announced his intentions to a crowd at the St. Cloud Hotel, stating that he had come to town with an olive branch in one hand and the Constitution in the other. While denying any hostility on his part, he stated that treason must be crushed and that traitors must be punished.

The "reconstruction" of Tennessee would be an obsession of Johnson's for the next 34 difficult months.

A Northern newspaper correspondent noted that "there is but little Union sentiment expressed here, in fact, far less than I had anticipated. All hands appear to hate us cordially."

(Continued on page 19)

Andrew Johnson, 17th U.S. President (1865-69)

A self-made man from humble origins, Johnson was working as a tailor in East Tennessee when he first embraced politics. Johnson rose from local politics to become a Congressman and Senator, Tennessee Governor, and the military governor of Tennessee during the Union occupation (1862-65). He was the only U.S. Senator in the South to refuse to resign when his state seceded.

As military governor, he dealt harshly with secessionists, demanding they take an oath of allegiance to the Union and imprisoning many who did not cooperate. Lincoln chose him as his running mate in the 1864 election. He served as Vice-President until the assassination of Lincoln in the spring of 1865. He then served as the country's 17th President until 1869. Politics were bitter following the war, and Johnson became the first of only two Presidents ever to be impeached. He died in 1875 and is buried in Greeneville, Tenn., at the Andrew Johnson National Historic Site.

Sam Davis, "Boy Hero of the Confederacy"

Sam Davis was born and raised on a farm in Smyrna, Tenn., southeast of Nashville. He attended Western Military Institute (Site 8) as a cadet and joined the Confederate army when the war began. Davis became an elite army scout (Coleman's Scouts, 1st Tenn. Infantry) at the age of 19. In November 1863 he was captured at Pulaski, Tenn. behind enemy lines with documents describing Union troop movements. He was taking the documents to Gen. Braxton Bragg at Chattanooga. Union Gen. Grenville Dodge offered to pardon him if he would divulge the source of the information. "If I had a thousand lives to live I would give them all gladly rather than betray a friend," Davis replied.

On Nov. 27, 1863, Davis was hanged by the U.S. Army. Ironically, the man the Federals wanted Davis to betray was already in custody. Davis is buried at his childhood home in Smyrna.

A statue of Sam Davis, by Belle Kinney, is located at the southwest corner of the Capitol grounds.

DOWNTOWN PARKING: During the week, visitors should park in paid lots or at street parking meters. On weekends, visitors may park free in the state employee parking lots to the west of the State Capitol.

All street metered spaces are free to the public Monday-Friday after 6 p.m. and Saturday after 12 p.m. and all day Sunday. (Some metered spaces may be reserved.)

Parking Lots
Parking Garages

The tomb of President and Mrs. James Knox Polk is located on the Capitol grounds. During the Civil War, the tomb was located at Polk Place, a couple of blocks from the Capitol, where Mrs. Polk lived.

Gen. Grant, who had earlier declared martial law, had paid his respects to Mrs. Sarah Polk, widow of President James K. Polk. She was said to have greeted him "with a polished coldness that indicated sufficiently in which directions her sympathies ran."

In the coming months Johnson told U.S. Army officials that before surrendering the city he would have it burned to the ground.

Enforcing the loyalty oath

When the mayor and city council refused to take an oath of loyalty to the state

"The city swarms with traitors, smugglers, and spies ... whose sole aim is to plot secret treason and furnish information to the rebel leaders."
—Federal authorities in Nashville

and federal Constitutions Gov. Johnson had the mayor arrested by the provost marshal. Then he fired most of the city's officials and replaced them with Unionists. John Hugh Smith replaced R.B. Cheatham as mayor. All city buildings were ordered to fly the Stars and Stripes.

Johnson met with local newspaper editors and laid out his rules. The editors

decided to cease publication.

The military governor arrested five Protestant ministers, who were some of the most ardent advocates of the Confederacy, and released them on their own recognizance. Five eventually were sent to prison at Camp Chase, Ohio.

In April, Johnson was shot at twice crossing Cedar Street from his residence to the State Capitol. A mounted guard was created to escort him in public.

On April 13, the *Daily Union* newspaper began publishing, edited by a loyal Unionist from Kentucky handpicked by Johnson. Two days later two local editors were arrested, charged with treason and imprisoned.

Most of those arrested were granted parole if they swore not to support the enemy and if they posted a $10,000 surety bond. If the parole was revoked, the offender might be sent to a Northern prison.

Secessionists sent to prison

Johnson hoped to convince the local populace to take the loyalty oath by making an example of several well-known secessionists. He arrested Gen. William Giles Harding, owner of Belle Meade, Gen. George Washington Barrow, and Judge Josepheus Guild, and imprisoned them at the state penitentiary. Then he sent them to Fort Mackinac in northern Michigan, where they spent countless hours watching Union soldiers march and drill. Four months later, Harding and Guild were paroled. Barrow was sent to Johnson's Island prison in Ohio and was exchanged in 1863.

In the city, there were rumors that all the members of the Confederate vigilance committee, which was keeping track of Unionists, would be arrested.

On April 12 it was rumored that the local "rebels" would rise at the peel of midnight bells and kill all the Union sympathizers. There were no incidents.

Citizens were prohibited from speaking to Confederate prisoners of war as they were marched through the streets.

By July, passes were required to enter or leave Nashville and only those taking the loyalty oath got passes. All U.S. soldiers were required to wear uniforms at all times or be regarded as deserters.

Wholesale arrests begin

When his plan to make examples of a few failed, Johnson began to make wholesale arrests, targeting bankers, insurance men, ministers, and doctors. The provost marshal rounded up 200 secessionists and put them in jail. Former governor Neill S. Brown and James Childress, the brother of Mrs. Polk, were arrested for treason.

The first of many mass meetings of Unionists was held at the Capitol, calling for restoration back into the Union.

A grand jury was impaneled by the Circuit Court and indicted some 50 men for conspiracy. Most of them had already left the city; those who hadn't took the loyalty oath.

All practicing attorneys and voters in local elections were required to take the

---

Parole of Honor:
I solemnly swear, without any mental reservation or evasion, that I will not take up arms against the United States, or give aid or comfort, or furnish information directly or indirectly to any person or persons belonging to any of the so styled Confederate States, who are now or may be in rebellion against the Government of the United States; so help me God.
It is understood that the violation of this parole is death.

---

loyalty oath. Those merchants who wanted to do business with the U.S. Army were required to take the oath. The army rewarded loyalists by posting guards to protect their property against vandals and thieves.

In June 1862, Johnson arrested 70 "vile secessionists" and exchanged them for loyal East Tennesseans held in jail in Mobile. He also sent eleven political prisoners to prison at Camp Chase, Ohio.

Local citizens defy authorities

Gen. John F. Miller, Nashville post commander, ordered the congregation of the Second Presbyterian Church to surrender their property to its Unionist members. It became the post church.

Father Emmeran Bliemel, pastor of the Church of the Assumption, was placed under surveillance and suspected of smuggling medicine to the Confederates. The U.S. Army police arrested Bliemel and found four ounces of morphine on his person. He denied the drugs were for the Confederates, and Gen. Rosecrans dismissed his case.

The daughter of the proprietor of the

St. Cloud Hotel was brought before Gov. Johnson by the provost marshal for spitting at Union officers from the porch of the hotel. Johnson let her go.

In August, Johnson assessed payments against 27 local businessmen to pay for the care of the city's indigent women and children. Several months later, 84 local residents were also taxed. By the end of the war, only about half of the assessments had been paid.

In Feb. 1863, Johnson issued the Confiscation Proclamation, stating that any property of the Confederate military or those in favor of rebellion was liable for confiscation by the U.S. Army.

In March 1863 a Board of Claims was created to investigate damages arising from occupation by U.S. troops. The claims were so numerous the board met every working day until October 1864.

Slavery divides local Unionists

A split among Nashville Unionists was caused when President Lincoln decided not to include Tennessee in the Emancipation Proclamation. Johnson emerged as a proponent of abolition and the leader of the "radicals." Conservatives and those Unionists who opposed the abolition of slavery rallied behind William Bowen Campbell.

The local police were ordered to confine runaway slaves and advertise in city papers so their owners could reclaim them. Exempt were slaves employed by the army and those owned by persons in states covered by the Emancipation Proclamation.

The City Council urged the mayor to impress runaway slaves (called contra-

---

Army Police Chief Abused His Official Powers

One of the most universally despised men in Nashville was William Truesdail, chief of the U.S. Army police, also known as the "secret police." His duties were to stop smuggling, limit the effectiveness of spies, gather intelligence, conduct counterintelligence, and police the loyalty of citizens and behavior of troops.

Truesdail abused his powers and feathered his nest with lucrative government contracts, including the supply of beef and the distribution of the mails. He bought cotton on speculation, using the name of his superior, Gen. Rosecrans, to gain favor. An investigation into such dealings cleared Truesdail.

In one incident, Truesdail arrested local merchant Jacob Bloomstein for smuggling, held him for four weeks in the state penitentiary and then had him sent to the prison at Alton, Ill. for three months. When he returned to Nashville, the contents of his store, including 3,000 pounds of cotton, had been stolen and his records destroyed.

When Truesdail was ordered in June 1863 to report to Murfreesboro a local newspaper noted that "nobody will regret the change" and called Truesdail "universally odious" to soldiers and citizens of both sides.

"The city swarms with a host of burglars, brass-knuck and slingshot ruffians, pickpockets, and highwaymen who have flocked hither from all parts of the country."

—**Nashville newspaper**

The State Capitol was fortified by the U.S. Army during the war and was called by some "Fort Johnson," after military governor Andrew Johnson.

(Courtesy of Tennessee State Library and Archives)

bands) into public works projects, street work, and other manual labor. Some officials urged Lincoln to begin enlisting blacks into the U.S. Army.

Union clubs were organized in Nashville. Nashville Union Club's 573 members met every Thursday night at the Capitol. They called for a convention to prepare for the holding of civilian elections. Separate registers were kept of the loyal and disloyal.

The *Daily Union* exhorted unmarried U.S. soldiers and officers "to hold fast to their integrity, and not permit themselves to be decoyed into matrimony by any she rebel, however fascinating and beautiful."

U.S. Army issues ultimatum

In April 1863 federal authorities began a crackdown, announcing in the newspapers that this time they were serious about the loyalty oath. More than 100 were arrested. Anyone who did not take the oath would be transported south of Union lines. Hundreds took the oath, waiting hours in line at the State Capitol. So many applied that the deadline had to be extended.

During May the provost marshal sent 25 sympathizers south each day.

On June 3, the *Daily Press* newspaper reported that 9,543 persons had taken the oath in the previous six months.

Beginnings of civilian government

In July 1863, Unionists from across the state met at the Capitol and pressed for state elections, resolving that only Unionists be able to vote, as well as Tennesseans in the U.S. Army.

In September, Lincoln instructed Johnson to re-inaugurate a loyal state government, confident that Tennessee was clear of "armed insurrectionists."

In December, Lincoln announced his Amnesty Oath, designed to encourage Southerners to return to their homes. Radicals thought the oath too lenient. In the first three months of 1864, more than 1,300 took the amnesty oath at Nashville. However, it was not uncommon to find guerillas who had signed copies of loyalty oaths on their persons.

By the beginning of 1864 Johnson was

mentioned as a candidate for higher federal office, even as Lincoln's vice-presidential running mate in the 1864 election.

In late January, however, Johnson shocked many by proclaiming that all voters in the March county election would subscribe to a stringent loyalty oath which included the extension of the Emancipation Proclamation to Tennessee. Johnson's oath was more stringent than Lincoln's amnesty oath.

Thousands refused to take Johnson's "Damnesty Oath." In an election newspaper editors called a farce, the Union candidates were elected 1,220 to 420.

Unionists campaign for president

In June, the Republican Party met in Baltimore and nominated the ticket of Lincoln and Johnson for the Nov. 8 presidential election. In Chicago, the Democrats nominated Gen. George McClellan and George Pendleton.

In the months before the election, the Union League and U.S. Army officials campaigned and rallied for the Lincoln-Johnson ticket while conservative Unionists favored McClellan.

The 10th Tennessee Infantry (US) held a rally at Fort Gillem to denounce those who attended the Chicago Democratic Party convention as "treasonable and a disgrace," and by a vote of 870-5 called for abolition of slavery, the perpetuation of the Union, and the election of Lincoln-Johnson.

The Nov. 8 election results were not known in Nashville for two days. The local

vote was 1,292 for Lincoln-Johnson and 25 for McClellan-Pendleton. A mock vote of blacks in the city favored Lincoln-Johnson by 3,193 to 1.

Civilian government established

Johnson still had much work to do before he left Nashville for Washington in late February 1865 to be inaugurated as U.S. Vice-President.

In January a Unionist convention proposed amendments to the state constitution, the abolishment of slavery, and nullified the state legislative acts of 1861. Also, the convention denied a request by local blacks seeking the right to vote. In February a referendum ratified those amendments overwhelmingly since only Unionists were allowed to vote. The vote in Nashville was 1,416 to 3.

On March 4, 1865, William "Parson" Brownlow was elected Governor along with the entire Union slate of candidates, the only candidates on the ballot.

On April 3, the state General Assembly convened in Nashville. News was received that Richmond, Va. had fallen to Union forces. Business was canceled. At noon the First Missouri Battery manned the guns at the Capitol and fired 100 rounds. The festivities continued into the night.

Two days later, Brownlow was inaugurated as Tennessee's civilian governor. The legislature ratified the 13th Amendment to the U.S. Constitution abolishing slavery.

In 1866 Tennessee was formally readmitted into the Union.

③ State Museum / War Memorial Plaza

The Tennessee State Museum is located at 505 Deaderick St., Nashville, TN 37243-1120, a short walk from the Capitol. The phone number is (615) 741-2692. Admission is free. Hours are Tues.-Sat., 10-5; Sun., 1-5. Closed Mondays and major holidays. The museum is located in the bottom level of the Polk Office Building and Tennessee Performing Arts Center. The main entrance is near Deaderick and 6th Ave. The museum includes a gift shop.

Civil War exhibits (subject to change) at the State Musuem include:

• Kepi and dogshead cane of CSA Gen. Patrick Cleburne

• Officer's coat of CSA Gen. John Adams

• Sam Davis' boot, which was cut open after he was captured by U.S. Army

• 1851 Navy Colt revolver owned by Gen. N.B. Forrest

• Brennan Foundry six-pounder cast-iron smoothbore cannon on carriage

• Musket, saber, and mittens of Confederate Gen. Felix Zollicoffer

• Brennan Foundry 12-pounder field howitzer (tube only)

• 12-pounder bronze Napoleon field artillery piece used by Gen. N.B. Forrest

• Flag of the 3rd Tennessee Volunteer Regiment captured at Fort Donelson, presented to Indiana Governor by the 44th Indiana Regiment and returned to Tennessee in 1962

• Battle flags of the 41st Tennessee, 14th Tennessee, and 5th Confederate Regiment

• Piece of hipbone from Confederate soldier embedded with bullet

• Saber of CSA Gen. James Rains

• Dress shirt of CSA Gen. John Hunt Morgan

• Saber of CSA Gen. Abraham Buford

• Battery flag and saber of Capt. J.W. Morton, Forrest's artillery commander

• Giant flag of the 10th Tennessee, Sons of Erin, Irish immigrants from Nashville

• Flag of Lebanon Greys, inscribed "Go And Fight"

• Diorama of Confederate field camp and artifacts

• Silk flag of the 32nd Tennessee Infantry Regiment

"Women of the Confederacy" statue by Belle Kinney is located at the southwest corner of War Memorial Plaza, which is directly across Charlotte Avenue from the State Capitol. Kinney (1890-1959) also sculpted statues of Andrew Jackson and Tennessee's first governor, John Sevier, which stand in Statuary Hall in the United States Capitol in Washington, D.C.

━━ Civil War Research Facilities (Public) ━━

Tennessee State Library and Archives
403 7th Ave. North, Nashville, TN 37243-0312
Call (615) 741-2764. Open Mon.-Sat., 8-6. Closed holidays.
Website: www.state.tn.us/sos/statelib/tslahome.htm
Located immediately west of the Capitol. Limited free parking available.

Nashville Public Library
615 Church St., Nashville, TN 37219
Call (615) 862-5800. Open Mon.-Thurs. 9-8; Fri. 9-6; Sat. 9-5; Sun. 2-5.
Website: www.library.nashville.org
Located on Church St. between 6th and 7th avenues. Parking garage entrance on 7th Ave.

| See Map on Page 19 |

St. Mary's Catholic Church

④

St. Mary of the Seven Sorrows Catholic Church at the corner of Charlotte Avenue and Fifth Avenue North is the oldest standing church in Nashville. The Greek Revival church was built in 1844-47 under the direction of Bishop Richard Miles, the father of the Catholic Church in Tennessee. He is buried in the chapel. There is some question as to the architect, either Adolphus Heiman or William Strickland.

At the time of construction the building was exemplary due to the lack of interior support columns. The stress beam that spans the width of the church remains as strong today as it was in 1847.

The church was used as a U.S. Army military hospital during the war. More than 300 men died on her floor.

Although now faced with stone, the entire building was brick during the 1860s and the circular arcade in the steeple was not enclosed as it is now.

For information about St. Mary's Church, call (615) 256-1704.

Nashville's Military Hospitals

Churches, public buildings confiscated to treat wounded

By the middle of 1863 there were 25 military hospitals in Nashville. The Cherry Street Baptist Church on Elm was used as the Post Hospital, with 125 beds. (The City Hospital had been destroyed by fire on Feb. 20, 1863, with all 240 patients safely evacuated.)

1.   Old gun factory, South Cherry St. on College Hill. Actually the College Hill Armory, the Third Presbyterian Church, and Primitive Baptist Church (60 beds)
2.   University building, South Market St. on College Hill
3.   Ensley buildings, SE corner of Public Square
4.   Howard High School, South College St. on College Hill
5.   Gun factory, upper end of Front Street
6.   College Street near Broad
7.   College Street between Church and Broad
8.   Masonic Hall and First Presbyterian Church, Church St. near Summer
9.   Carriage factory, North Market St. below the Public Square
10.   Medical College, South College Street
11.   Pest House on University Pike
12.   Broadway Hotel, Broad St. between Cherry and Summer
13.   Hume High School, South Spruce Street and corner of Broad
14.   Nashville Female Academy, Church St. near Chattanooga Depot
15.   Hynes High School, Line St. at corner of Summer
16.   Gordon Block, corner of Broad and Front
17.   Planters Hotel, officers hospital, North Summer corner of Deaderick
18.   Corner of Church and College
19.   Morris and Stratton Building, No. 14 North Market St.
20.   First Baptist Church, North Summer St. between Deaderick and Union
21.   McKendree Methodist Church, Church St.
22.   H.S. French & Son, corner of Clark and Market
23.   Corner of Vine and Broad
24.   Prison hospital, Second Baptist Church, South Cherry St. on the Hill
25.   Convalescent barracks, Maxwell House, corner of Cherry and Church

Nashville in 1864

1. **State Capitol. Built 1845-59. Designed by William Strickland in Greek Revival design. Occupied by military Governor Andrew Johnson, the building was fortified with palisades, parapets, and heavy field artillery. Also known as Fort Johnson. National Historic Landmark.**

2. Adelphi Theatre. Built in 1850 by noted local architect Adolphus Heiman with second largest stage in America.

3. Hicks Building (1857), No. 46 Public Square. Italianate building of Harvey Akeroyd design occupied by dry goods and readymade clothing companies. Used by Federals to store ordnance.

4. Morgan Building, No. 49 Public Square. Dry goods and clothing company. Used by Federals to store ordnance.

5. Douglas Building, No. 53 Public Square. Four-story building of Douglas & Co., dry goods and readymade clothing merchant. Used to store ordnance.

6. Union Hotel.

7. Inn Block. Site of old Nashville Inn which burned in 1856. Clothing merchants, druggists, grocer, liquor store and book bindery located here. Federals used buildings as medical storage and commissary storage.

8. Public Square. Center of public life in Nashville.

9. City Hall and Market. Redesigned by Adolphus Heiman in 1855.

10. Courthouse (1857). Designed by Francis Strickland, it was similar in design to State Capitol except it did not have a tower. Located in Public Square it was site of many mass gatherings.

11. Southern Methodist Publishing House. Established 1854 when church split over slavery into northern and southern factions. Taken over by Federals and used to print army forms and reports.

12. City Hotel

13. Suspension Bridge. Span of 700 feet connected Nashville with Edgefield across the Cumberland. Wood flooring burned by fleeing Confederates in Feb. 1862. Site of Woodland St. bridge. Pillars of bridge can still be seen.

14. Pontoon Bridge. Built in Oct. 1862 on empty ice barges at middle ferry landing. Another bridge was built in Dec. 1864 in severe winter weather over which Wilson's cavalry rode from Edgefield camps.

15. Steamboat Landing.

16. Ensley Building. Five-story Italianate building used by Federals as part of Hospital No. 3, with 200 beds.

17. Watson House hotel. Used in connection with Hospital No. 19.

18. Morris Stratton & Co. Four-story brick building housing wholesale grocers. Used by Federals as part of Hospital No. 19, containing 300 beds.

19. French & Co. Three-story brick building used as part of Hospital No. 19.

20. Nashville & Chattanooga Railroad Depot. Included castellated passenger depot, roundhouse, repair shop, brass shop, copper shop, supply houses, print shop and coal yard capable of holding four million bushels.

21. Nashville Female Academy. Used in conjunction with Hospital No. 14.

22. Polk Place (1818-20) at Union and Vine was home of the widow of President James K. Polk and site of the President's tomb, designed by William Strickland. The tomb is now located on the State Capitol grounds.

23. Felix DeMoville House. Built in 1857, two-story brick house with hipped roof served as Gen. Rousseau's headquarters in 1864.

24. George W. Cunningham House on High St. Elegant Renaissance-Revival. Used by Federal commanding generals as their headquarters, including Grant, Sherman, Thomas, Buell, and Rosecrans.

25. New Theatre. Located in the Odd Fellows Grand Lodge.

26. Zollicoffer House. Townhouse on High Street used as Provost Marshal's Office. Located at current TPAC site. Owner Felix Zollicoffer was a Nashville Whig newspaper editor. At Logan's Crossroads in 1862 he was the first Confederate general killed in the western theater. He is buried at City Cemetery.

27. **St. Mary's Catholic Church. Extant. Built 1844-47 by Heiman or Strickland. The oldest standing church in Nashville.**

28. Architect Adolphus Heiman's townhouse (1850).

29. Planter's Hotel. Federals used it as Officers' Hospital No. 17 and as the Soldiers' Home by the U.S. Sanitary Commission.

30. First Baptist Church. Built 1841 by Heiman, it featured tall, slender twin spires. Used by Federals as military hospital, containing 150 beds.

31. Bank of Tennessee. Built 1853 by Francis Strickland, modeled after father's Second Bank of the U.S. in Philadelphia. Used by Federals as paymaster's department building. Exact location uncertain; corner of Cherry and Union.

32. Christ Episcopal Church. Built 1829-31 by Hugh Roland.

33. St. Cloud Hotel. One of the city's finest hotels and temporary quarters of several Union generals.

34. James Stevenson's stoneyard (gravestones).

35. Masonic Hall. Four-story brick building built 1860 by Heiman. Second-story auditorium used for theatrical events. Used by Federals as part of Hospital No. 8, it had 368 beds.

36. Maxwell House Hotel. Begun in 1859 by John Overton, Jr. Used by Confederates as Zollicoffer Barracks and later by Federals as a prison for captured Confederates.

37. McKendree Methodist Church. Site of famous 1850 convention on Southern secession. Used by Federals as part of Hospital No. 21.

38. **First Presbyterian Church. Completed 1851 by William Stickland, the brick church features two square towers. Now known as Downtown Presbyterian Church. One of the nation's finest examples of Egyptian Revival architecture. Used by Federals as part of Hospital No. 8, containing 206 beds. Extant. National Historic Landmark.**

39. E.H. Ewing & Co. Approximate location. Wholesale grocers used as carpenter's shop by Federal army.

40. Cumberland Presbyterian Church. Part of Hospital No. 8, it had 41 beds.

41. Hume School (1855). City's first public school building. Built by Heiman in castellated Gothic style. Federals quartered railroad employees in it.

42. Dr. John Shelby's Medical College opened 1858 with 85 students but closed during the war and never reopened. An indigent hospital adjoined the structure, which included a teaching hospital.

43. Nashville & Decatur Railroad Depot.

44. Taylor Depot. Commissary warehouse on Nashville & Decatur RR. Burned down in June 1865.

45. Broad Street Fire Company No. 2. Approximate location. Firehall and engine house featuring a bell tower topped by statue of fireman.

46. Brennan Foundry. Cannon tubes were cast here for the Confederacy before the Federals shut down the facility. Ironwork on the tower of the State Capitol was cast here.

47. City Hospital. Destroyed by fire in February 1863. Later site of huge Federal underground gunpowder magazine.

48. **Elm Street Methodist Church. At Summer Street. Brick with tall steeple and spire. Extant, now office building.**

49. University Medical Department. Classes were held here throughout the war. Used in conjunction with Hospital No. 10.

50. Howard School. Built 1860 by Harvey Akeroyd. Three-story brick with Italianate clock tower. Located northwest of current building with same name.

51. Rutledge House. Also known as Rose Hill, home of Henry and Septima Rutledge. Burned near end of war.

52. University of Nashville Faculty Housing. Used as part of U.S. military hospital No. 2.

53. **Western Military Academy. Built 1853-54 as Literary Building for University of Nashville, limestone building was used as military institute, then used as part of Hospital No. 2, with 300 beds.**

54. Lindsley Hall. Built 1855 by Adolphus Heiman as university dormitory, used by both sides as military hospital. Three-story, castellated brick building. Its two hundred beds were reserved for Federal officers.

55. Factory (teamsters' quarters). Three-story brick building with wooden shingle roof and openable skylights.

56. City Water Works.

Boldface indicates structures still standing.

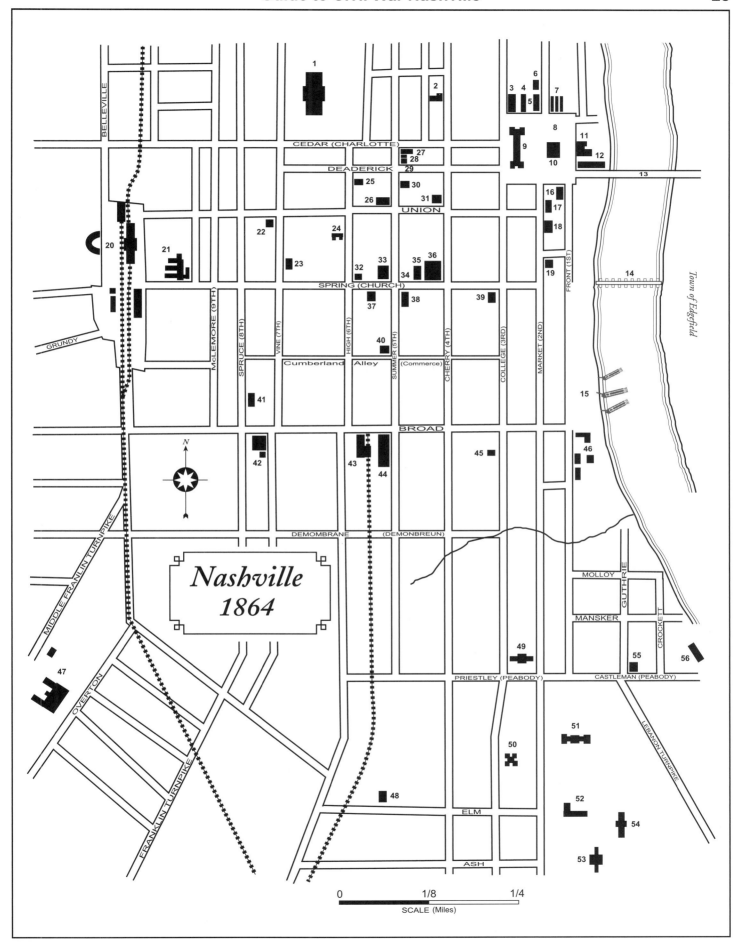

Nashville 1864

(5)
Downtown Presbyterian Church

National Historic Landmark

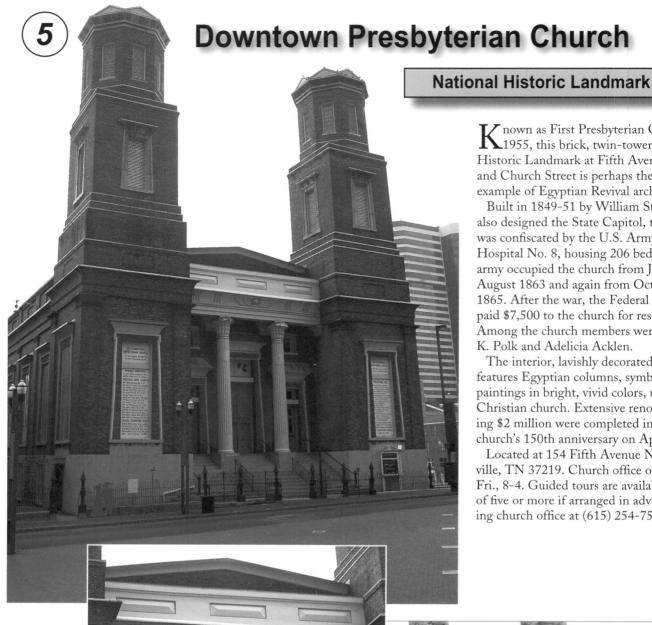

K nown as First Presbyterian Church until 1955, this brick, twin-towered National Historic Landmark at Fifth Avenue North and Church Street is perhaps the world's finest example of Egyptian Revival architecture.

Built in 1849-51 by William Strickland, who also designed the State Capitol, the building was confiscated by the U.S. Army and used as Hospital No. 8, housing 206 beds. The Union army occupied the church from January to August 1863 and again from October 1863 to 1865. After the war, the Federal government paid $7,500 to the church for restorations. Among the church members were Mrs. James K. Polk and Adelicia Acklen.

The interior, lavishly decorated in the 1880s, features Egyptian columns, symbols, and paintings in bright, vivid colors, unusual for a Christian church. Extensive renovations costing $2 million were completed in time for the church's 150th anniversary on April 29, 2001.

Located at 154 Fifth Avenue North, Nashville, TN 37219. Church office open Mon.-Fri., 8-4. Guided tours are available for groups of five or more if arranged in advance by calling church office at (615) 254-7584.

Detail of Egyptian Revival features.

First Presbyterian Church as it appeared in 1864. James Stevenson's stoneyard is across the street.

(Courtesy of Tennessee State Library and Archives)

Nashville Visitors Center
Broadway at Fifth Avenue • (615) 259-4747

The Nashville Visitors Center is located in the glass tower at the Gaylord Entertainment Center (the "GEC") on Broadway at Fifth Avenue. Open daily, the center offers brochures and maps, discounted attraction tickets, help with reservations and itinerary planning, a small museum display, and a gift shop.

Nashville is located in the Central Time Zone.

Important telephone numbers:
Nashville Convention and Visitors Bureau
 (615) 259-4700 and 1-800-657-6910 • www.nashvillecvb.com
Nashville Chamber of Commerce
 (615) 743-3000 • www.nashvillechamber.com
Emergency police, fire or ambulance • 911
Non-emergency police dept. • (615) 862-8600
Non-emergency fire dept. • (615) 862-5421
Tennessee Highway Patrol • (615) 741-2060

Underground Railroad Terminal
102 5th Ave. South

This small brick building is possibly the oldest building in downtown Nashville, built in 1810. During the years preceding the Civil War, this house reportedly served as a Nashville terminal within the "underground railroad," which aided slaves in their attempts to flee to freedom in the North. The building, which now houses a commercial business, is located near Broadway and Fifth Avenue South, across the street from the Nashville Visitors Center.

(6)

Holy Trinity Episcopal Church

Union troops used Holy Trinity Episcopal Church as a powder magazine and horse stable, causing much damage and delaying the building of the tall slender tower until 1887. Built of rugged limestone with a large square tower and taller octagonal turret, the church's Gothic Revival architecture is reminescent of an English parish church. It was one of 17 churches built in South Nashville, which was annexed by Nashville in 1854.

Today, the beautiful country church sits surrounded by a commercial and light-industrial section of the city just south of downtown.

For information about touring the church, call (615) 256-6359.

(7) # Elm Street Methodist Church

The Elm Street Methodist Church was used as a military hospital after the Battle of Nashville. Today the building houses architectural offices and lacks its 19th century bell tower and tall steeple.

It is not open to the public for tours.

Western Military Institute • Hospital No. 2

This collegiate, Gothic-style building was designed by Nashville architect Major Adolphus Heiman and was built in 1853-54 as the Literary Department of the University of Nashville. Shortly thereafter, it became the site of Western Military Institute, where Gen. Bushrod Johnson taught military science and Cadet Sam Davis attended classes. At the outbreak of war, all of the cadets joined and fought for the Confederacy.

During the Union occupation of the city, the limestone building became Hospital No. 2, housing 300 beds. There were 25 Federal military hospitals in Nashville, occupying churches, schools, and other significant structures. Fourteen thousand wounded were brought to Nashville after Shiloh, and 60 to 100 died each day in the hospitals here. One entire room was set aside for "dead-men's knapsacks."

The limestone building measured 175 by 50 feet and had a composition roof. It was built to house the Literary Department of the University of Nashville but the department failed economically and was converted to the military department of the school.

More than twice as many men died of disease during the war than from battlefield wounds. Medical treatment was relatively primitive and sanitary conditions often were poor. The foundations of many hospitals, such as this one, had a lime-based whitewash applied to them in the belief that it would prevent contagion.

The building, located at 724 Second Avenue South, now houses the Metro Nashville Planning Commission and is not open for public tours.

Prostitution legalized, regulated by U.S. Army in Nashville to prevent disease

During the war, hundreds of prostitutes came to Nashville to ply their trade. Venereal disease reached epidemic proportions among the U.S. Army soldiers stationed in or near the city.

On July 6, 1863, Gen. Robert Granger, the post commander, ordered all prostitutes out of the city. Three hundred to four hundred were rounded up, forced onto steamboats at the wharf, and sent to Louisville. Black prostitutes were exempt from Granger's order, for unknown reasons. By the end of July, the prostitutes were returning. By Aug. 4, one steamboat, shunned by every city on the river, returned to Nashville.

Granger rescinded his order and accepted the recommendation of the Provost Marshal that prostitution, in effect, be legalized and regulated. Prostitutes were ordered to be examined by U.S. Army surgeons for venereal disease. Those free of disease were granted a license by the Provost Marshal to conduct business. By August 21, at least 360 prostitutes had been licensed. Infected prostitutes were treated in a hospital building on the western city limits that had previously been used for smallpox patients. Later, Hospital No. 11 on University Pike, once a pest house, was converted into a second hospital for prostitutes. Nearly a thousand cases of venereal disease had been diagnosed among prostitutes the first six months of 1864.

By Sept. 1, 1864, the U.S. Army had licensed 460 prostitutes in Nashville.

(9) Confederate Circle at Mount Olivet Cemetery

Confederate Circle (1869) at Mt. Olivet Cemetery (1856), marked by a 45-foot-tall monument (1889), is the final resting place of approximately 1,500 Confederate soldiers killed in battles in Middle Tennessee. Seven CSA generals are buried at or near the circle: William B. Bate, William N.R. Beall, Benjamin Franklin Cheatham, William H. Jackson, George E. Maney, James E. Rains, and Thomas Benton Smith. Nearby are the graves of Col. Adolphus Heiman and Col. Randall McGavock.

Confederate Circle at Mt. Olivet Cemetery is owned by the United Daughters of the Confederacy. A brochure for a walking tour of the cemetery is available at the cemetery office.

Confederate Memorial Hall

Gen. William B. Bate monument

Marker to unknown Confederate soldiers

Key to Numbered Gravesites on Page 31:

1.-Confederate Memorial Hall is a converted holding crypt containing interpretive panels of information and pictures about local Southern military heroes and personalities. Maintained by the Joseph Johnston Camp of the Sons of Confederate Veterans.

2.-Confederate Circle holds the graves of 1,500 soldiers in 13 rows encircling the 45-foot-tall granite monument. The first six rows are graves of Confederates from outside Tennessee; the seventh row is unknown soldiers; the outer rows are Tennesseans. The burial ground was dedicated in 1869 by the Ladies Memorial Society. The monument was unveiled May 16, 1889 with 10,000 persons present.

3.-Brig. Gen. Thomas Benton Smith, who was captured at Shy's Hill (Site 23) and assaulted by Col. William McMillan. Struck thrice on the skull with a sword, Smith was not expected to live. He died in 1923 at the age of 85, having spent most of his years after the war in an insane asylum.

4.-Acklen vault, an impressive Gothic structure, holds the remains of Adelicia Acklen, mistress of Belmont Plantation (Site 14), two of her three husbands, five of her six children, and one grandchild. Inside is Peri, a statue which once graced Belmont's Grand Salon.

5.-Col. David C. Kelley, the "Fighting Parson," who fought under Forrest and whose cavalrymen, armed with light artillery, fought off Union gunboats on the Cumberland River west of Nashville from Dec. 2-15, 1864.

6.-Gen. William Hicks "Red" Jackson commanded a division of cavalry under Forrest in late 1864. After the war he married Selene Harding, daughter of Gen. William Giles Harding, and managed Belle Meade Plantation (Site 24) for many years, making it the top-ranked thoroughbred horse farm in the South.

7.-Brig. Gen. James Edwards Rains, a Nashvillian who was killed at the Battle of Stones River, Dec. 31, 1862, leading his men against a Union battery. First buried at City Cemetery, he was moved here in 1888.

Acklen Vault

8.-John Bell of Nashville served as Secretary of War and as a U.S. Senator before running for President in the 1860 election won by Abraham Lincoln. Against secession, he won three states—Tennessee, Kentucky and Virginia—on the Constitutional Union party ticket. Although he later sided with the South, he played no role in the hostilities.

9.-John W. Morton, originally of the Rock City Guards (Nashville's prewar militia), served as Gen. N.B. Forrest's chief of artillery.

10.-Gen. Alvan C. Gillem, a West Point graduate, was one of only six Tennesseans who served as Union generals during the war. He served as quartermaster under Thomas and Buell early in the war and then as Provost Marshal of Nashville. In June 1863 he was appointed adjutant general of Tennessee.

11.-Major Gen. William B. Bate of Tennessee was severely wounded at Shiloh, recovered, and went on to command at all battles of the Army of Tennessee from Dalton, Ga. to Greensboro, N.C. His division was overwhelmed at Shy's Hill (Site 23) on Dec. 16, 1864. He later served as Governor and U.S. Senator.

12.-Vernon King Stevenson was "Father of Tennessee Railroads" and president of the Nashville and Chattanooga R.R. He fled the city on a special train during the Great Panic of 1862, abandoning his duties as city quartermaster.

13.-Carter masoleum. Built by Daniel F. Carter, wealthy banker and stagecoach owner, to house the remains of his son, John Carter, a Confederate soldier killed at Perryville, Ky.

14.-Brevet Gen. Gates P. Thruston of the U.S. Army married the daughter of prominent Nashvillians after the war and later wrote the definitive book on Tennessee archaeology.

15.-Major General Benjamin Franklin Cheatham of Nashville fought in every major battle of the Army of Tennessee. His corps held the right flank on the first day of the Battle of Nashville, but lost the left flank the following day. He later became Postmaster of Nashville.

16.-Brig. Gen. William N.R. Beall surrendered with his brigade at Port Hudson, Miss. in July 1863 and was imprisoned, later paroled to serve as an agent for the relief of CSA prisoners in Northern camps.

17.-Gen. William Giles Harding of Belle Meade Plantation (Site 24) was arrested by military governor Johnson for his support of the Confederate army. He was imprisoned at Fort Mackinac, Mich. from April-Sept., 1862 and then paroled.

18.-Gen. George E. Maney of Franklin, Tenn. commanded the 1st Tennessee Regiment and fought in battles from Shiloh to Atlanta. He ran for governor after the war and had diplomatic posts in South America.

19.-Judge John Overton, owner of Travellers Rest (Site 21), died in 1833. He helped found the city of Memphis.

20.-Col. Randal W. McGavock, former mayor of Nashville, commanded the 10th Tennessee Regiment. He was killed at the Battle of Raymond, Miss., May 1863, leading his Irish Confederates.

21.-John Catron, first Tennessean to serve on U.S. Supreme Court, was a Unionist who fled Nashville when the state seceded and returned after the Union occupied the city.

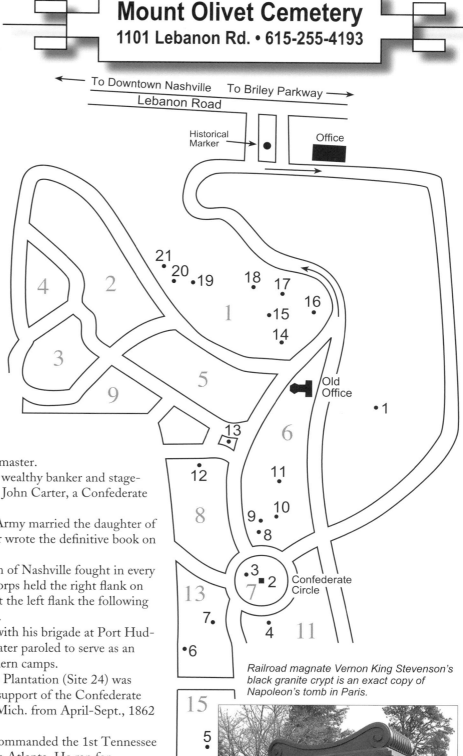

Mount Olivet Cemetery
1101 Lebanon Rd. • 615-255-4193

Railroad magnate Vernon King Stevenson's black granite crypt is an exact copy of Napoleon's tomb in Paris.

Granbury's Lunette

Granbury's Lunette at 190 Polk Avenue was a small fort holding the far right of the Confederate line when the Battle of Nashville began on Dec. 15, 1864. The fort was manned by the 334 men, mostly Texans, of Granbury's Brigade under Capt. Edward Broughton (Gen. Hiram B. Granbury had been killed at Franklin). The entire Confederate right wing was under command of Maj. Gen. Benjamin F. Cheatham.

The battle was commenced at 6 a.m. when Maj. Gen. James B. Steedman attacked the Confederate right flank in what was a diversionary, holding movement. The Federal force, which included several U.S. Colored Troops regiments, was repulsed soundly, with heavy losses. Many men were killed when they fled into the steep railroad cut to the southwest (the railroad cut immediately next to the lunette site was excavated in the 20th Century and probably demolished a portion of the lunette). Cheatham fell back southward to a secondary line at about 9 p.m.

The site is owned by the Gen. Joseph Johnston Camp of the Sons of Confederate Veterans and located adjacent to McCord Crane Co., which helped save the site.

City Cemetery

Gravesite of Capt. William Driver.

Gravesite of Gen. Felix Zollicoffer.

The Nashville City Cemetery (established 1822) at 1001 Fourth Avenue South and Oak St. was the initial resting place for Union and Confederate soldiers who had died in military hospitals of wounds suffered at battles such as Shiloh and Stones River. More than 14,000 soldiers poured into Nashville's hospitals after Shiloh, and up to 100 per day died at the hospitals despite treatment. W.R. Cornelius was the official undertaker in Nashville and buried soldiers from both sides in the open field southwest of the cemetery, each grave marked with a wooden headboard. Unfortunately, the headboards disappeared during the war, probably used for firewood.

After the war, the U.S. soldiers were moved to National Cemetery and many of the Southerners were moved to Mt. Olivet Cemetery.

Buried here is Capt. William Driver, a former New England sea captain who sailed around the world several times. A staunch Unionist, he retired to Nashville, where his brother lived. Capt. Driver had nicknamed his seafaring flag "Old Glory" and hid it from local secessionists after Tennessee entered the Confederacy. When Union troops marched into Nashville in late February 1862, Capt. Driver retrieved the flag, which had been stitched into a bedcover, and personally hoisted Old Glory on a staff above the main entrance of the State Capitol. News spread, and over time the American flag came to be known as Old Glory. The captain's flag is now at the Smithsonian Institution in Washington, D.C.

The Civil War produced divided loyalties among its citizenry. Three of Capt. Driver's sons fought for the Confederacy, and one was killed in battle.

Key to numbers on City Cemetery map on Page 33:
1-Capt. Driver's gravesite.
2-Gen. Felix K. Zollicoffer of Nashville was the first general to be killed in the Western Theater, at the battle of Fishing Creek, Ky. on Jan. 19, 1862. A newspaper editor and Whig politician, he had served as a state senator and a U.S. Congressman. He had urged loyalty to the Union but sided with Tennessee when the state seceded.
3-White Turpin, 22, a Mississippian in Darden's Battery, died one month after being wounded at the Battle of Nashville. He was buried by his family apart from the other soldiers.
4-Wartime site of Union and Confederate soldier burials.
5-Gen. Richard S. Ewell of Virginia fought in the Eastern Theater, lost a leg at Second Manassas and commanded Stonewall Jackson's old division at Gettysburg. In 1863, he married Lizinka C. Brown of Nashville and retired to Spring Hill, Tenn. after the war where he operated a prosperous farm.
6-Gen. Samuel Reid Anderson was a native Virginian and son of a Revolutionary War soldier. He served in the Mexican War and was Postmaster of Nashville, 1853-61. He served as Junior Major General of Provisional Forces of Tennessee

City Cemetery

in 1861. He served mostly in the Eastern Theater.

7-Marker for Brig. Gen. James E. Rains of Nashville. He was killed at the Battle of Stones River (Murfreesboro) in January 1863 and buried at City Cemetery. Later he was moved to Mt. Olivet Cemetery.

8-Gen. Bushrod Rust Johnson was a professor at Western Military Institute before the war. His wife was buried at City Cemetery in 1858. During the war, he was captured at Fort Donelson, and was the hero at the Battle of Chickamauga, leading Longstreet's troops through the gap in the Union lines. He was buried in his native Ohio upon his death in 1880. In the 1970s his remains were reburied at City Cemetery with full military honors. He now lies beside his wife.

9-Lt. Andrew W. Gould, a student of Professor Bushrod Johnson, was killed in an altercation with his commanding officer, Gen. Nathan Bedford Forrest, in Columbia, Tenn. on June 26, 1863. *Exact site of burial unknown.*

Gravesite of Gen. Richard Ewell.

Gravesite of Gen. Bushrod Johnson.

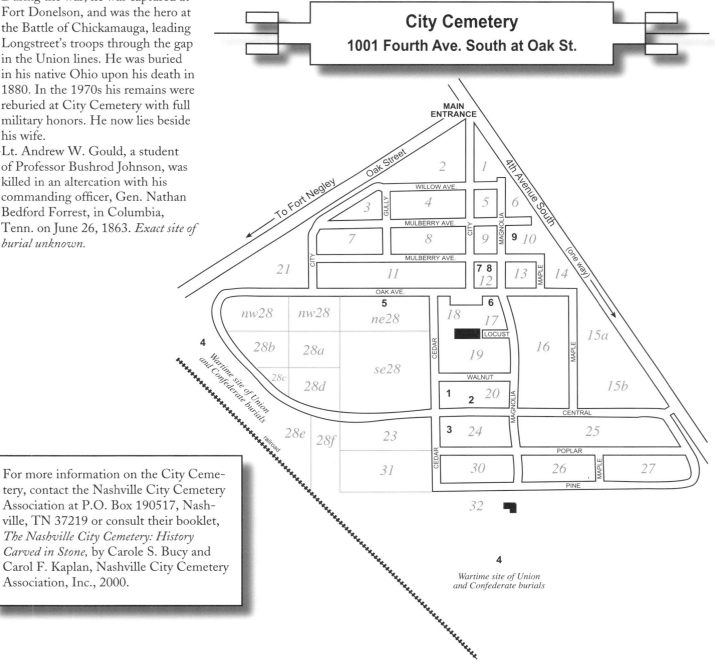

For more information on the City Cemetery, contact the Nashville City Cemetery Association at P.O. Box 190517, Nashville, TN 37219 or consult their booklet, *The Nashville City Cemetery: History Carved in Stone,* by Carole S. Bucy and Carol F. Kaplan, Nashville City Cemetery Association, Inc., 2000.

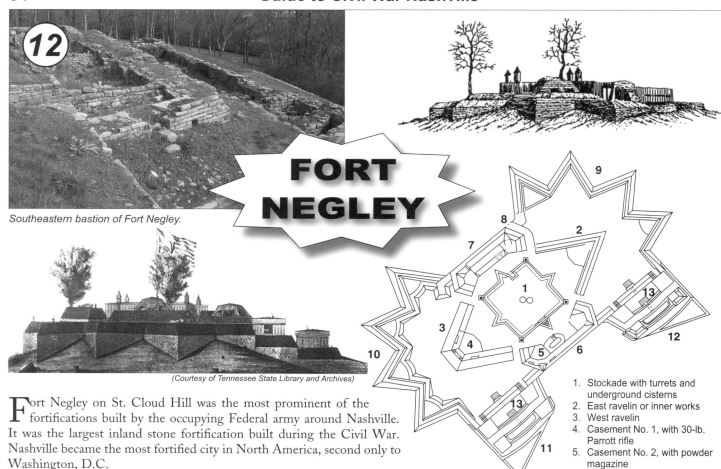

Southeastern bastion of Fort Negley.

(Courtesy of Tennessee State Library and Archives)

1. Stockade with turrets and underground cisterns
2. East ravelin or inner works
3. West ravelin
4. Casement No. 1, with 30-lb. Parrott rifle
5. Casement No. 2, with powder magazine
6. South main works
7. North main works
8. Main entrance gate
9. East outer parapets with redans
10. West outer parapets with redans
11. Southwest artillery bastion
12. Southeast artillery bastion
13. Bastion tunnels

Fort Negley on St. Cloud Hill was the most prominent of the fortifications built by the occupying Federal army around Nashville. It was the largest inland stone fortification built during the Civil War. Nashville became the most fortified city in North America, second only to Washington, D.C.

The design by U.S. engineer Gen. James St. Clair Morton is elaborate, star-shaped, and European in origin. The fort was named for U.S. Gen. James S. Negley, provost marshal and commander of Federal forces in Nashville.

The fort was built largely by black laborers from October to December 1862. Contrabands (runaway slaves) and free blacks were impressed by the army to build the 23 fortifications around the city.

Fort Negley is 600 feet long, 300 feet wide, and covers four acres. It used 62,500 cubic feet of stone and 18,000 cubic feet of earth. At the southern end of the fort, where attack was most likely, were two massive, bombproof bastions equipped with guns which could be aimed in several directions. Each bastion had tunnels which protected men moving through the works.

Casement No. 1 protected a 30-pound Parrot rifle, a cannon which could hurl a 29-pound shell 2.5 miles. There were 11 guns in the fort, operated by 75 artillerymen.

The opening shots of the Battle of Nashville on Dec. 15, 1864, were fired from Fort Negley, although the fort itself was never directly attacked at any time during the war.

After the war, the fort was abandoned and allowed to deteriorate. During the 1930s, WPA work crews reconstructed the remains, but those works also fell into disrepair.

Fort Negley Park is located on St. Cloud Hill at the southeast corner of the intersection of I-65 and I-40 near Adventure Science Center. Following improvements by City of Nashville Parks, the fort opened to the public in 2004 for the first time in 60 years. Extensive interpretive signage and elevated walkways allow self-guided tours during daylight hours. There is no admission fee.

Looking southwest from Fort Negley, the City Reservoir (arrow points to pumphouse) can be seen on the horizon. The wartime site of Union Blockhouse Casino would have been to the left of the reservoir.

LEFT: Fort Negley was fully restored during the 1930s by public works crews, as evidenced in this aerial view taken from the southeast. At that time, as at the time of the battle, St. Cloud Hill was void of trees, unlike today. Unfortunately Fort Negley was again allowed to fall into disrepair, prompting renewed committments to restore the historic site and open it to the public.

(Courtesy of Ross Massey)

RIGHT: Casement No. 1 at Fort Negley was a railroad-iron-plated bomb-proof holding a 30-pound Parrott rifle capable of hurling shells a distance of two miles. The big guns fired salvos into Hood's Army of Tennessee to open the Battle of Nashville, Dec. 15, 1864.

BELOW: A view of the defensive lines of Nashville during the Battle of Nashville, Dec. 15-16, 1864, after the U.S. troops had advanced beyond their staging areas and attacked the Army of Tennessee. In the distance on the hilltop is Blockhouse Casino, viewed from the direction of Fort Negley. Franklin Pike runs diagonally across the view.

(Courtesy of Tennessee State Library and Archives)

(Library of Congress)

U.S. Army Defenses of Nashville - 1864

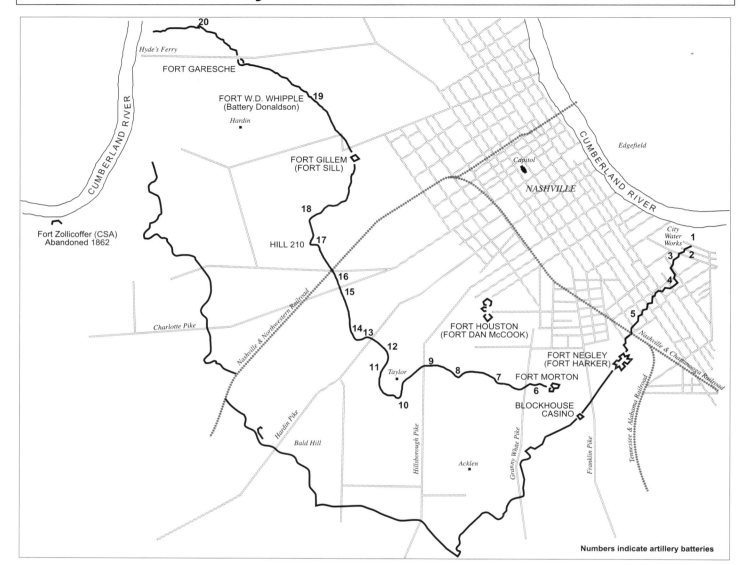

Numbers indicate artillery batteries

Nashville, a vital city which had barely been fortified by the Confederates in 1861, became under Union occupation the most heavily fortified city in North America, second only to Washington, D.C. Holding Nashville in Federal hands was imperative, the military governor arguing that the city be burned to the ground rather than fall into Confederate hands again.

Nestled in a bend of the Cumberland River, major portions of Nashville were protected by this natural barrier and the ironclad Union gunboats which patrolled it.

Shortly after the city's capture, the Union forces placed batteries at barricades controlling the eight roads into the city—the Lebanon, Murfreesboro, Nolensville, Franklin, Granny White, Hillsboro,

Harding and Charlotte turnpikes. The guns were placed so that they could easily be turned against the city itself in case of a civilian uprising.

Under orders from Gen. Buell, Capt. James St. Clair Morton, chief engineer of the Army of the Ohio, began work on three main forts—**Fort Negley** on St. Cloud Hill, **Fort Morton,** and **Fort Houston.**

Using impressed labor, slaves, and mules, Fort Negley was built in 1862-64 as an impressive defensive work, the largest inland stone fort built during the war (see page 34 for more details). Late in the war, Fort Negley was renamed Fort Harker in honor of a general killed in action.

Across Franklin Pike was Fort Morton, another large and complicated structure situated on solid limestone (current loca-

tion of Rose Park).

Further south was **Blockhouse Casino** on Kirkpatrick Hill, now occupied by the City Reservoir. A large cross-shaped blockhouse was constructed there which could be defended, if necessary, by guns at Fort Negley and Fort Morton.

The third fortification, Fort Houston, was built on high ground near the current Music Row traffic roundabout. The home of prominent Union loyalist Russell Houston was destroyed to built the fort named after him. Later it was renamed Fort Dan McCook.

Work progressed slowly at Forts Morton and Houston due to the lack of labor and the complex design of the structures.

About this time, Capt. Morton placed earthen parapets and a log stockade at the State Capitol at the urging of Military

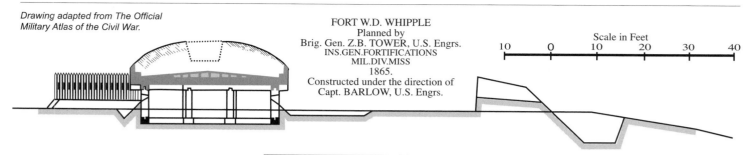

Drawing adapted from The Official
Military Atlas of the Civil War.

FORT W.D. WHIPPLE
Planned by
Brig. Gen. Z.B. TOWER, U.S. Engrs.
INS.GEN.FORTIFICATIONS
MIL.DIV.MISS
1865.
Constructed under the direction of
Capt. BARLOW, U.S. Engrs.

Scale in Feet
10   0   10   20   30   40

Gov. Andrew Johnson. **Fort Johnson,** as it came to be known, was armed with 15 heavy guns and a regiment of infantry.

The railroad bridge across the Cumberland River was fortified with guardhouses and stockades with loopholes so that infantry on the bridge could shoot at any attackers. The modifications required 40,000 board feet of heavy timbers.

Nine heavy guns were set on the bank of the river for defense of the eastern part of the city.

"Each prominent street is barricaded, and beautiful homes have been relieved of their roofs and turned into forts or rifle pits, and the fort on St. Cloud Hill, which commands the town and surrounding country has been made of such strength that it can scarcely be taken," wrote a Louisville newspaper correspondent.

In May 1864, a grand depot magazine was completed at the center of an eight-acre field where the city hospital had been located prior to burning down in early 1863. The rectangular underground structure measured 65 feet by 200 feet and was covered with earth eight feet thick. The magazine was supplied by a branch railroad line built on a trestle. The depot was well-ventilated and virtually waterproof. Citizens were relieved to have gunpowder stored outside the city limits.

In October 1864, under the direction of Gen. Zealous B. Tower, Army engineer, revised plans for the defensive fortifications of Nashville were submitted to Washington. Original plans were simplified so that work could resume on the forts.

With the approach of the Confederate Army of Tennessee in November 1864, work by laborers, soldiers, and quartermaster employees commenced on both the inner and outer defensive lines and continued around the clock.

The inner defensive line was seven miles long and contained 20 batteries of heavy guns. Encompassing the city and all significant Federal works, the line would be manned by a garrison of 3,000 soldiers supported by 2,000 mobile troops plus

Forts were named for Union commanders, officers

Col. Julius Garesche, chief of staff to Major Gen. William S. Rosecrans, was killed at the Battle of Stones River in Murfreesboro, Dec. 31, 1862. He was decapitated by a cannon ball while riding with the general, who was rallying the troops.

William Denison Whipple (1826-1902) of New York became Gen. Thomas' chief of staff in Dec. 1863. After the war he served as aide-de-camp to General-in-Chief W.T. Sherman. He is buried in Arlington National Cemetery.

Bvt. Brig. Gen. James L. Donaldson was a Lt. Colonel in Nov. 1863 when named senior and supervising quartermaster for the Department of the Cumberland, stationed in Nashville. His men manned the inner defenses during the Battle of Nashville.

Brig. Gen. Alvan Cullem Gillem (1830-75) was a native of Gainesboro, Tenn., one of only six native Tennesseans to serve as Union generals. He served as quartermaster to Gen. Thomas and Gen. Buell early in the war. As Colonel of the 10th Tennessee Infantry he served as Provost Marshal of Nashville. In April 1865 he became a member of the state legislature. He is buried at Mt. Olivet Cemetery.

Brig. Gen. Joshua Woodrow Sill (1831-62) of Ohio was a West Point classmate of Schofield and Hood. He was killed in combat at Murfreesboro, Dec. 31, 1862, leading one of Sheridan's brigades. He is buried near Chillicothe, Ohio.

Russell Houston, a local Union loyalist, was named to the state Supreme Court in 1864 by Military Governor Andrew Johnson.

Brig. Gen. Daniel McCook, Jr. (1834-64), one of the "Fighting McCooks" of Ohio, was mortally wounded leading the charge of Davis' Division, Army of the Cumberland, against Confederate fortifications on Kennesaw Mountain, Ga., on June 27, 1864. He died July 17 in Ohio. He is buried in Spring Grove Cemetery, Cincinnati, Ohio.

Major James St. Clair Morton (1829-64) of Philadelphia, Pa. was a brilliant student and 1851 West Point graduate who was posted to the Corps of Engineers. In June 1862 he became chief engineer of Gen. Buell's Army of the Ohio and in April 1863 he became chief engineer of Gen. Thomas' Army of the Cumberland and architect of Nashville's defensive fortifications. He also commanded the Pioneer Brigade of engineers under Gen. Rosecrans. He was killed in front of Petersburg on June 17, 1864, and posthumously promoted to brevet brigadier general. He is buried in Laurel Hill Cemetery, Philadelphia.

Major Gen. James Scott Negley (1826-1901) of Pennsylvania served in Gen. Buell's army and was posted in Nashville to defend the city while Buell chased Bragg into Kentucky in late 1862. He served well at the battle of Stones River and the Tullahoma Campaign but was charged with cowardice at the Battle of Chickamauga. Although cleared of charges, he resigned in Jan. 1865 and subsequently served several terms in Congress. He is buried in Allegheny Cemetery, Pittsburgh.

Brig. Gen. Charles Garrison Harker (1835-64) of New Jersey was a West Point graduate who fought at Shiloh, Perryville, and Murfreesboro, and helped Gen. Thomas defend Snodgrass Hill at the Battle of Chickamauga. He was killed in combat leading a brigade in Newton's Division, Howard's Corps, Army of the Cumberland at Kennesaw Mountain, June 27, 1864. He is buried in Swedesboro, N.J.

4,000 quartermaster employees and could repel a force of up to 30,000 men.

The inner works began at the Cumberland River at the water works (current site of the old General Hospital), and ran across University Hill to Fort Negley. From Fort Morton it ran westward to a strong salient at the Taylor farm (current site of Vanderbilt University). Then it ran northerly (along the eastern boundary of the current Centennial Park) to a fortification known as **Hill 210** (current site of Washington School). Here was placed two bastion fronts for 15 cannons, supported by rifle pits.

The next large fort was **Fort Gillem** (later renamed Fort Sill) located at the current site of Jubilee Hall on the Fisk University campus. It was built by the 10th Tennessee Regiment, commanded by Gen. Alvan Gillem. It was a redoubt 120 feet

Continued on Page 44

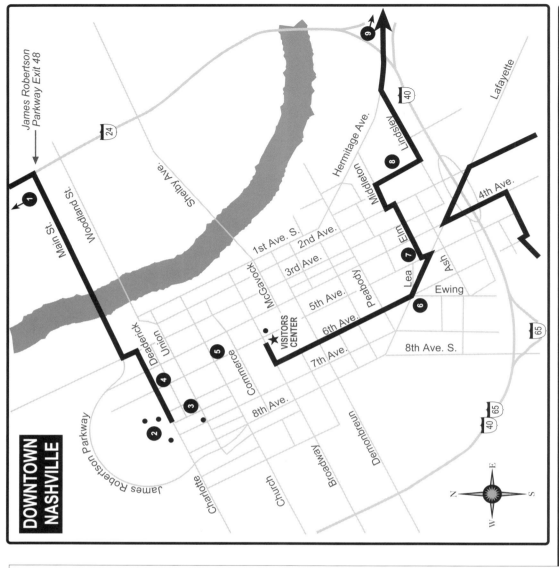

Key to Civil War Nashville Driving Tour Sites:

1 National Cemetery-Page 16-GPS N36° 14.505' / W86° 43.412'

2 State Capitol-Page 18-GPS N36° 09.930' / W86° 46.979'

3 State Museum/War Memorial Plaza-Page 22-GPS N36° 09.874' / W86° 46.972'

4 St. Mary's Church-Page 23-GPS N36° 09.957' / W86° 46.911'

5 Downtown Presbyterian Church-Page 26-GPS N36° 09.984' / W86° 46.819'

6 Holy Trinity Episcopal Church-Page 28-GPS N36° 09.206' / W86° 46.911'

7 Elm Street Methodist Church-Page 28-GPS N36° 09.165' / W86° 46.408'

8 Western Military Institute-Page 29-GPS N36° 09.235' / W86° 46.092'

9 Mt. Olivet Cemetery-Page 30-GPS N36° 09.214' / W86° 44.027"

10 Granbury's Lunette-Page 32-GPS N36° 08.002' / W86° 44.933'

11 City Cemetery-Page 32-GPS N36° 08.941' / W86° 46.164'

12 Fort Negley-Page 34-GPS N36° 08.584' / W86° 46.572'

13 Blockhouse Casino-Page 34-GPS N36° 08.392' / W86° 46.710'

14 Belmont Mansion-Page 46-GPS N36° 08.120' / W86° 47.707'

15 Sunnyside-Page 47-GPS N36° 07.281' / W86° 47.423'

16 Battle of Nashville Monument-Page 47-GPS N36° 06.853' / W86° 47.562'

17 Redoubt No. 4-Page 48-GPS N36° 06.233' / W86° 49.567'

18 Redoubt No. 1-Page 48-GPS N36° 06.919' / W86° 48.452'

19 Old Monument Site-Page 48-GPS N36° 06.745' / W86° 46.429'

20 Peach Orchard Hill-Page 65-GPS N36° 05.210' / W86° 46.318'

21 Travellers Rest-Page 65-GPS N36° 04.446' / W86° 46.012'

22 Stewart's Stone Wall-Page 66-GPS N36° 05.197' / W86° 47.484'

23 Shy's Hill-Page 66-GPS N36° 05.271' / W86° 48.500'

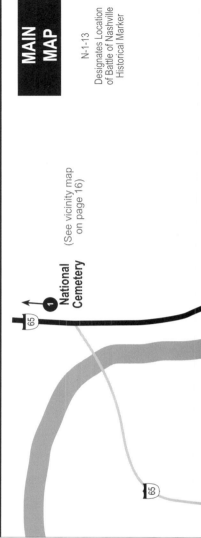

DOWNTOWN NASHVILLE

James Robertson Parkway Exit 48

MAIN MAP

N-1-13

Designates Location of Battle of Nashville Historical Marker

(See vicinity map on page 16)

National Cemetery

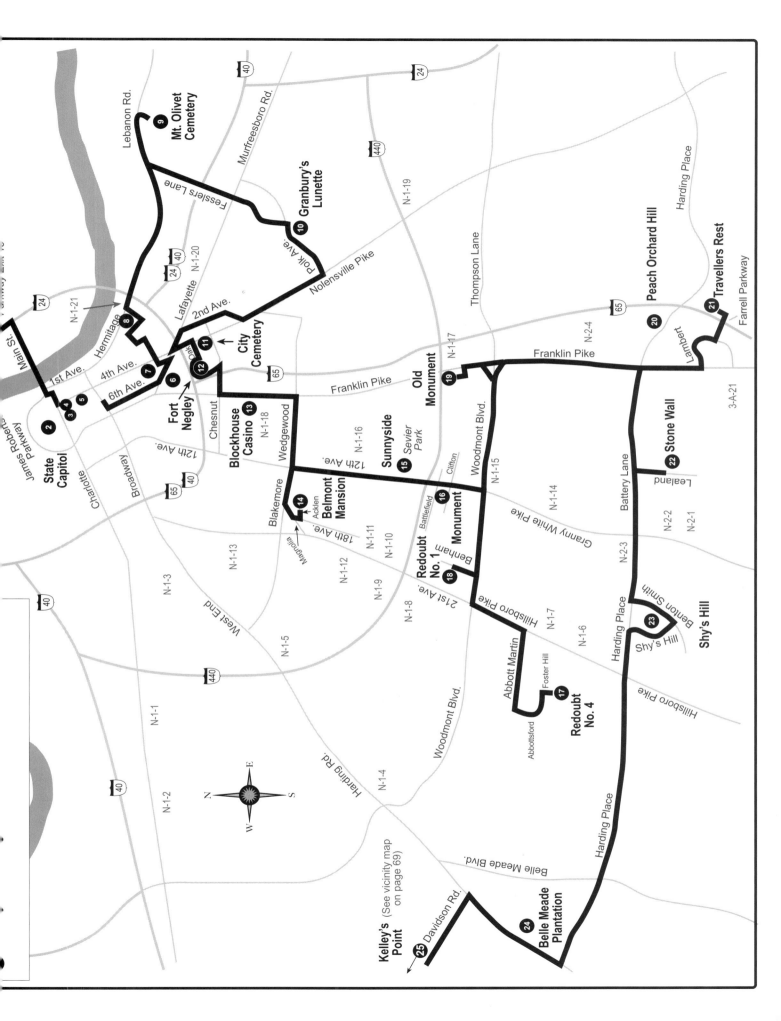

Directions for Driving Tour of Civil War Nashville

Refer to maps on pages 38-39

Please drive carefully. A driver and navigator is strongly recommended. You will be driving through heavily congested urban streets. Road conditions may vary. Be aware that some routes are known by two or more names. Familiarize yourself with the tour sites and photographs in advance so that you know what to look for. Drive at your own risk.

Although the tour route is numbered and sequential, you can pick and choose which sites you wish to visit. For example, Tour Site No. 1 is optional but very accessible for those traveling to Nashville from the north. Please see vicinity maps for Tour Sites 1 and 25. The entire 50-mile tour will take most of the day if you choose to take all or most of the guided tours featured at some of the tour stops.

From southbound I-65 north of Nashville take Exit 90B Briley Parkway-Opryland (Route 155) and proceed 1.5 mi. eastward to Exit 14A Gallatin Road (Hwy. 31E North) and drive 0.5 mi. north to entrance of **National Cemetery (Tour Site No. 1: Page 16)** on the left. Refer to cemetery map on page 17.

Backtrack to I-65 South and drive 5.3 miles south to Exit 48 James Robertson Parkway-State Capitol (along the way keep to the leftbound interstate lanes, continuing on East I-24/East I-40 (Chattanooga-Knoxville).

Turn right onto James Robertson Parkway, which will take you over the Cumberland River on Victory Memorial Bridge and into downtown Nashville. Turn left at 3rd Ave. North and then an immediate right onto Charlotte Ave. **St. Mary's Church (Tour**

non Road another 1.5 mi. to entrance of Mt. Olivet **Cemetery (Tour Site No. 9: Page 30)** on your right. After entering, turn left, drive past cemetery office, and follow map on page 31.

Backtrack on Lebanon Road to Fesslers Lane and turn left. Drive two miles to Polk Ave. and turn right. After 0.2 mi. and immediately after driving over the railroad cut will be **Granbury's Lunette (Tour Site No. 10: Page 32)** on your left. Park next door at private business (McCord).

Continue on Polk Ave. for 0.4 mi. and turn right onto Nolensville Rd. Note mileage. The road will split into one-way routes, you will go through a very narrow and short railroad tunnel and you will now be on 2nd Ave. South. in a residential area. After driving 2.5 mi. turn left at an angle onto Lafayette Ave., also known here as Murfreesboro Rd. (Rt. 41/70S). Do not turn hard left onto McCann! Drive under several interstate highway overpasses and at the next traffic light, turn left onto 4th Ave. South (one-way street). Drive back under the interstate overpass and the entrance to **City Cemetery (Tour Site No. 11: Page 32)** will be one block on your right at Oak St. intersection. See cemetery map on page 33.

From the cemetery, turn left onto Oak St. At 6th Ave. South intersection bear right and then left onto Bass St. following sign to Science Center. Drive over railroad and around the science center. Behind the science center is **Fort Negley (Tour Site No. 12: Page 34)**. The entrance is a large stone gate to your left.

Backtrack to Abbott Martin Rd. and turn right. Turn left at Hillsboro Pike and then turn right at Woodmont Blvd. In 0.2 mi. turn left onto Benham and drive 0.1 mi. to the top of the hill and **Redoubt No. 1 (Tour Site No. 18: Page 48)** on your left. Park carefully.

Backtrack to Woodmont Blvd. and turn left. Drive 1.8 mi. and exit right to Franklin Rd. (Rt. 31). Turn left onto Franklin Rd. Drive under highway and 0.1 mi. later turn left at Greenbriar Apts./Villa Adrian. Before entering complex, turn right onto short access road, and the **Old Monument Site (Tour Site No. 19: Page 48)** is one block straight ahead.

Backtrack to Franklin Rd. and turn right. Note mileage. At 0.4 on your left is Glen Leven, a private antebellum mansion not open to the public. Go 1.2 mi. to the intersection with Battery Lane (Rt. 255). To your left is the area of **Peach Orchard Hill (Tour Site No. 20: Page 65)**. Note this intersection because you will return here. Note mileage. Continue south on Franklin Rd. for 0.6 mi. and turn left onto Lambert, just past Overton High School. Turn left at stop sign onto Farrell Parkway. Drive under the interstate and railroad and turn left into entrance of **Travellers Rest (Tour Site No. 21: Page 65)**.

Backtrack to Franklin Rd. and turn right. Drive north 0.5 mi. to Battery Lane (Rt. 255) and turn left. Drive west on Battery Lane for

Site No. 4: Page 23) is two blocks on your left and the **State Capitol (Tour Site No. 2: Page 18)** is three blocks to your right. There is a convenient parking lot (fee) at the northeast corner of 5th Ave. North and Charlotte, across from St. Mary's.

Most of the tour stops in downtown Nashville (Tour Sites Nos. 2 to 5) are within walking distance of the State Capitol, although you may wish to drive to the Visitors Center on Broadway.

From the **Visitors Center**, drive west on Broadway one block to 6th Ave. South and turn left. (The tall gray, stone tower ahead of you on the south side of Broadway is the U.S. Customs House–photo on page 70.) Drive six blocks to Lafayette St. Across the street at Ewing is **Holy Trinity Episcopal Church (Tour Site No. 6: Page 28)**. Church tours must be arranged in advance.

Turn left onto Lafayette, drive one block and turn left onto 5th Ave. South and proceed straight onto Elm St. at the site of **Elm St. Methodist Church (Tour Site No. 7: Page 28)**. The church is now a private business and not open to the public.

Drive three blocks to 2nd Ave. South (one-way street) and turn left. Drive less than a block and turn right onto Middleton St. At the top of the hill turn right at the sign for Children's Theatre and County Clerk onto unnamed private street. **Western Military Institute (Tour Site No. 8: Page 29)** will be about one block on your left.

Continue on unnamed street to Lindsley Ave. and turn left. Drive four blocks to Hermitage Ave. and turn right. Note your mileage. You will drive under highway overpasses and through a light industrial area. This road now becomes Lebanon Road. In a little over a mile, take note of Fesslers Lane to your right (you will be returning here). Continue on Leba-

Continue to Chesnut St. and turn right. Proceed over the interstate and turn left at the next traffic light at 8th Ave. South (which further south becomes Franklin Pike). Two blocks on your right is the City Reservoir (closed to public), the war-time site of **Blockhouse Casino (Tour Site No. 13: Page 34)**.

At the next traffic light, turn right onto Wedgewood. Note mileage. After 0.6 mi. note 12th Ave. South intersection but drive straight through (you will return here). Two blocks later you will see Belmont University on your left. At second stoplight, turn left onto Magnolia Blvd. One block later, at 18th Ave. South, turn left and then immediately turn left onto Acklen. **Belmont Mansion (Tour Site No. 14: Page 46)** entrance is one block straight ahead.

Backtrack to 12th Ave. South (right onto 18th Ave., right onto Magnolia, right onto Wedgewood) and turn right. Note mileage. After driving 1.1 mi. through small commercial area turn left onto Kirkwood and enter Sevier Park. **Sunnyside Mansion (Tour Site No. 15: Page 47)** is just beyond parking area.

Turn left onto 12th Ave. South and drive over I-440 (overpass with stone walls). The route now becomes Granny White Pike. Just past the overpass to your right is the **Battle of Nashville Monument (Tour Site No. 16: Page 47)**. Turn right at Clifton into parking area.

Continue south on Granny White Pike two blocks to Woodmont Blvd. traffic light and turn right. Note mileage. At 0.9 mi. turn left at traffic light onto Hillsboro Pike. In 0.6 mi., just past The Mall at Green Hills, turn right onto Abbott Martin Rd. Drive 0.8 mi. and turn left onto Abbottsford Dr. Drive slowly for 0.5 mi. and turn right onto Foster Hill Dr. At the end of the street is **Redoubt No. 4 (Tour Site No. 17: Page 48)**.

1.1 mi. and turn left at traffic light onto Lealand Lane. Drive 0.2 mi. to metro historical marker and **Stewart's Stone Wall (Tour Site No. 22: Page 66)** on your left.

Backtrack to Battery Lane and turn left. Drive 1.0 mile (Battery Lane becomes Harding Place) and turn left onto Benton Smith Rd. Proceed up hill 0.1 mi. to historical marker and steps on your right to **Shy's Hill (Tour Site No. 23: Page 66)**. Park carefully. Steps to the top are very steep.

Continue on Benton Smith Rd. to first road on your right, Shy's Hill Rd., and drive short distance back to Harding Place and turn left. Drive 3.6 mi. to Harding Rd. (Rt. 70S) and turn right. Drive 0.4 mi. on Harding Rd. to entrance to **Belle Meade Plantation (Tour Site No. 24: Page 68)** on your right.

Exit Belle Meade Plantation, turn right onto Leake Rd. and at Harding Rd. intersection turn right. Drive 0.8 mi. and turn left at traffic light onto Davidson Rd. Note mileage. Refer to vicinity map on page 69. After 1.7 mi. you will need to veer left, staying on Davidson Rd. in order to reach Charlotte Pike, which you will reach in 1.3 mi. Turn left onto Charlotte Pike and then shortly turn right onto unnamed road leading to **Kelley's Point park "JDN Greenway" (Tour Site No. 25: Page 69)**.

This concludes the Civil War Nashville driving tour. We hope you have enjoyed your visit and come back soon.

BATTLE of NASHVILLE HISTORICAL MARKERS

All markers are titled "Battle of Nashville," with appropriate subtitles. Markers are listed as they occur on streets and highways leading out of Nashville, from west to east.

Unfortunately, many markers are difficult to read due to traffic conditions and lack of suitable parking. Some are missing due to construction projects or vandalism.

Numbers match those on the map on Page 39. The text can be read to understand where units were positioned and how the battle flowed on each day.

(Note: The serial numbers on each marker are for administrative purposes only and have no historical value.)

N-1-2
Cavalry Action
Dec. 15, 1864

The right of the main Federal defense line crossed Charlotte Pike here. In the opening phase of the battle, mounted and dismounted cavalry of Wilson's 6th Cavalry Corps moved out of the Federal works, supporting the advance of Smith's XVI Corps in a turning movement against the extreme left flank of the Confederate positions.

Location: Charlotte Avenue, between 33rd and 35th avenues.

N-1-1
Cavalry Action
Dec. 15, 1864

Forming the outer arc of the main Federal attack, R.W. Johnson's 6th Cavalry Division, Wilson's Corps, here hit Rucker's Confederate Cavalry Brigade, west of Richland Creek. Withdrawing southward to Harding Road, Rucker held his ground there until bypassing Federal infantry forced further withdrawal to Hillsboro Pike late in the afternoon.

Location: 54th Avenue, west of Richland Creek Bridge

N-1-3
Federal Defenses

The hill to the west was a strong point in the system of permanent Federal defenses, started in 1862, which extended to the river on both sides of town. Artillery was emplaced here from time to time.

Location: West End Avenue, in Centennial Park, near the Parthenon

N-1-5
XVI Corps Line of Departure
Dec. 15, 1864

Supported by a division of Wilson's cavalry, A.J. Smith's Corps moved westward astride Harding Road, displacing Ector's Confederate Brigade from positions across the pike northward to the west of Richland Creek. This brigade outposted the

sions of Loring and Walthall holding fast until the XVI Corps, moving past their left, forced withdrawal.

Location: 21st Avenue South, at Cedar Lane

N-1-9
Redoubt No. 1
Dec. 15, 1864

Stewart's Confederate Corps held this salient of the left of Hood's defenses. A thin infantry line ran south behind a stone wall on the east side of the pike. After the routing of Ector's Brigade on Harding Pike and successive overrunning of Redoubts 3, 4, and 5 to the south, Stewart's position was flanked; he withdrew southeast toward Granny White Pike.

Location: TN 106 (Hillsboro Pike), near intersection with Hampton Avenue

N-1-8
Confederate Outpost
Dec. 15, 1864

100 yards west was Redoubt No. 3 in the Confederate system of detached works beyond the main line. It was overrun by the enveloping attack of Wood's IV Corps from the northwest.

Location: TN 106 (Hillsboro Pike), south of intersection with Woodmont Boulevard

N-1-7
Lumsden's Defense
Dec. 15, 1864

0.3 mile west was Redoubt No. 4 in Hood's detached supporting works. Garrisoned by Lumsden's Battery of smoothbore Napoleons, supported by 100 men of the 29th Alabama Infantry under Capt. Foster, it was finally overrun by the assault of 12 infantry and 4 dismounted cavalry regiments, supported by four Federal batteries.

Location: TN 106 (Hillsboro Pike), at Hobbs Road

Location: Granny White Pike, at Harding Place

N-2-2
Smith's Assault
Dec. 16, 1864

The Federal XVI Corps attacked southward along this road. After violent artillery bombardment, McArthur's Division took the hill to the west about 4:00 p.m., precipitating the route of Hood's Army. This hill is named for Col. W.M. Shy, 20th TN Inf., killed in the desperate defense which he commanded.

Location: Granny White Pike, between Harding Place and Sewanee Road

N-2-1
Confederate Position
Dec. 16, 1864

Stewart's Corps, badly mauled during the first day, withdrew at night to a line extending eastward. Lee's Corps, forming the right wing, extended the line across the Franklin Pike. Cheatham's Corps, on Stewart's left, extended the line westward, and following the hills, curved south. Chalmers' Cavalry Division covered the left flank.

Location: Granny White Pike, at Sewanee Road

N-1-18
Federal Defensive Line
Dec. 15, 1864

The Federal defensive line ran NE and SW through here. Ft. Casino was on the hill to the west, Fort Negley to the northeast. Garrisoned on Dec. 2 by Schofield's XXIII Corps, it was occupied by Cruft's Provisional Division when the battle began. The XXIII Corps moved out in support of the main effort, 5 miles southwest.

Location: 8th Avenue South, on south slope of hill below City Reservoir

N-1-17
Lee's Position
Dec. 15, 1864

Here, Stephen D. Lee's Corps, Army of Tennessee, bestrode the highway and railroad. Cheatham's Corps held the right of the line, which ran northeast about 2 miles to Rains' Hill. After the Confederate left was broken in the afternoon's fighting, Lee's Corps fell back to high ground about 1 1/2 miles south.

Location: TN 6 (Franklin Pike), near Thompson Lane

N-2-4
Confederate Defenses
Dec. 16, 1864

Lee's Corps held the right flank of the line in the final stages

of the battle, linking with Stewart to the west. Here it extended east, then south around Peach Orchard Hill. Violent attacks by Steedman's brigades were repulsed bloodily; Lee did not withdraw until the left and center of the Confederate line had collapsed.
Location: TN 6 (Franklin Pike), north of intersection with Elysian Fields Road

N-1-19
Cheatham's Line
Dec. 15, 1864

Holding a line running NE and SW and with its right on the N.C. & St. L. R.R. at Rains' Cut, Cheatham's Confederate Corps stood off the attacks of Steedman's brigades. Part of Cheatham's Corps was moved to the support of Stewart's line late in the afternoon; collapse of the left wing forced Cheatham's withdrawal southward during the night.
Location: 4th Avenue South, at Peachtree Street

N-1-21
Steedman's Line of Departure
Dec. 15, 1864

The left of the Federal main defensive line rested on the Cumberland River north of here, extending southeast to the Murfreesboro Pike. From this line, Steedman's Provisional Detachment of six brigades made the secondary attack against the Confederate right. Thomas' main attack was delivered against the Confederate left.
Location: Hermitage Avenue, near entrance to the old General Hospital

N-1-20
Steedman's Position
Dec. 15, 1864

From a line of departure running NE-SW through here, Maj. Gen. Steedman's Provisional Detachment of 6 brigades at 6:00 a.m. launched a holding attack southwestward against the Confederate right, on high ground about 2 miles south. The main attack, about 5 miles west, enveloped the Confederate left after an all-day fight.
Location: Lafayette Street, at Claiborne Street

3-A-21
Hood's Retreat
Dec. 16, 1864

In this neighborhood, late in the evening of his decisive defeat at Nashville, Hood reorganized his army for withdrawal southward. Lt. Gen. Stephen D. Lee's Corps, supported by Chalmers' Cavalry Division, covered the withdrawal, fighting continuously until the army bivouacked near Spring Hill, 21 miles S., the night of Dec. 17th.
Location: U.S. 31 (Franklin Pike), Davidson County, near Brentwood

Source: *"Tennessee Historical Markers," Tennessee Historical Commission, 1996*

Confederate left flank; the main line was along Hillsboro Pike.
Location: West End Avenue, at Orleans Drive

N-1-4
Defense by Ector's Brigade
Dec. 15, 1864

In position from here northward along high ground, Ector's Brigade of French's Confederate Division, commanded by Col. Daniel Coleman, outposted the left of Hood's line. Attacked by the Federal XVI Corps, supported by artillery and part of the Cavalry Corps, it was overwhelmed. It withdrew southeast to Hillsboro Pike.
Location: West End Avenue, at Ridgefield Avenue

N-1-13
Federal Defenses
Dec. 2-15, 1864

Near here, the interior defensive lines ran southwest to cross Harding Pike; the total length of these works was about 7 miles. First garrisoned by Wood's IV Corps, it was occupied Dec. 15 by Donaldson's Division of Quartermaster employees. Part of the breastworks can be seen on Vanderbilt campus, 300 yards west.
Location: 21st Avenue South, at entrance to Vanderbilt Campus

N-1-12
Outer Federal Defenses
Dec. 2, 1864

Here the outer Federal defensive line, which stretched 7 miles around the city, crossed Hillsboro Pike. It was used as the commencement of battle on Dec. 15 by Wood's IV Corps as a line of departure for the main attack. Faint traces of the old entrenchments are visible a few yards west.
Location: 21st Avenue South, at Bernard Avenue

N-1-11
IV Corps Drop-Off Line
Dec. 15, 1864

Using the defensive salient 500 yards east, Wood's Corps, with the XVI Corps on its right, swung southwest to envelop the left of the Confederate line, 1 1/2 miles south, and pushed it back in spite of determined resistance. The XXIII Corps (Schofield) followed in support.
Location: 21st Avenue South, at Linden Avenue

N-1-10
Assault on Montgomery Hill
Dec. 15, 1864

500 yards east of here, Maj. Gen. T.J. Wood led an assault by his IV Corps against the Confederate skirmish line on the hill, eventually carrying it. Attacking the main line about 600 yards south, Wood was unable to take it by direct assault, the divi-

N-1-6
Taking of Redoubt No. 5
Dec. 15, 1864

Hood's Redoubt No. 5 was on this hill. Couch's division of the XXIII Corps, sweeping to the south of the route of Smith's XVI, captured it and the hills to the east late in the afternoon. Wilson's cavalry, crossing the highway about 2 miles south, advanced rapidly eastward, flanking the Confederate defenses.
Location: TN 106 (Hillsboro Pike), 0.8 mile south of marker N 17

N-1-16
Schofield's Jump-Off Line
Dec. 15, 1864

The Federal defensive line ran northeast and southwest through here. It was garrisoned by Schofield's Corps on arrival here after the Battle of Franklin, Dec. 2, and later became a line of departure for the advance into support positions: Cruft's Provisional Division then occupied this line in reserve.
Location: 12th Avenue South, south of intersection with Acklen Avenue

N-1-15
Confederate Defenses
Dec. 15, 1864

Stewart's Corps, Army of Tennessee, held this part of Hood's original line, extending east about 1500 yards, and west and south about 1 mile to Hillsboro Pike. After the turning of his left, about 4:00 p.m., Stewart established a new position extending southward, to the west of Granny White Pike.
Location: Granny White Pike, near intersection with Woodmont Boulevard

N-1-14
Confederate Defenses
Dec. 15, 1864

After being outflanked by the advance of the Federal XVI Corps (Smith), Loring and Walthall put their divisions in a defensive line west of this road, facing westward. Here, their determined defense brought Federal advances against the Confederate left to a close for the day.
Location: Granny White Pike, near intersection with Shackleford Road

N-2-3
Schofield's Assault
Dec. 16, 1864

The Federal XXIII Corps attacked southeastward from positions about 3/4 mile west. Coordinating with the attack of Smith's XVI Corps, and assisted by pressure by Wilson's encircling cavalry from the south, its action brought about the final collapse of Hood's defenses.

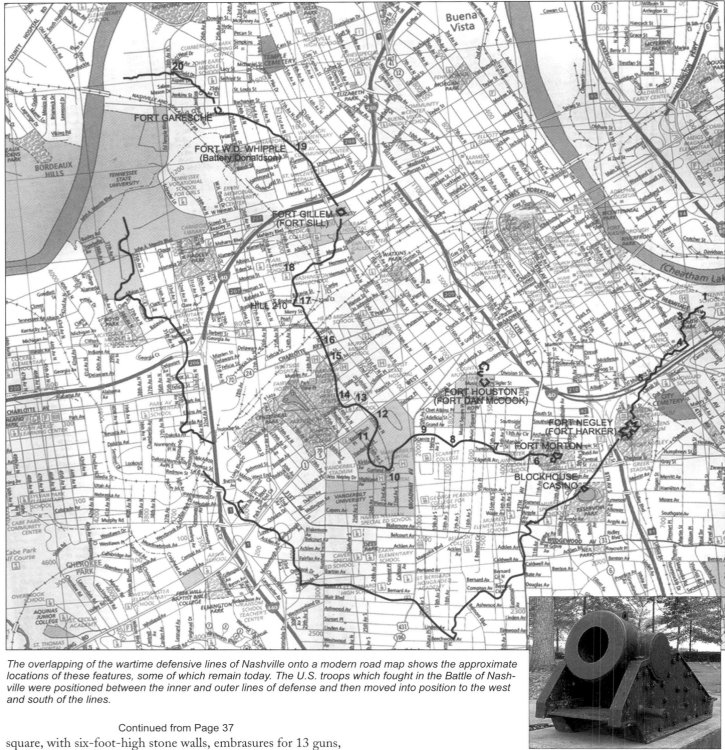

The overlapping of the wartime defensive lines of Nashville onto a modern road map shows the approximate locations of these features, some of which remain today. The U.S. troops which fought in the Battle of Nashville were positioned between the inner and outer lines of defense and then moved into position to the west and south of the lines.

One of two Union mortars on Tip Top Hill in the northwestern portion of Centennial Park on West End Avenue.

Continued from Page 37
square, with six-foot-high stone walls, embrasures for 13 guns, two service magazines, and a blockhouse.

A mile north of Fort Gillem was **Fort Garesche,** built by the 2nd Ohio Volunteers and housing 14 guns and three magazines. It was located at the present intersection of Buchanan St. and 26th Ave. Between Fort Gillem and Fort Garesche was **Battery Donaldson** (aka Fort W.D. Whipple), a small battery with an octagonal bombproof blockhouse.

Beginning at Blockhouse Casino and diverting from the inner lines was the outer line of defense, also running west to the bend in the Cumberland River. The distance between the inner and outer lines ranged from half-a-mile to a mile.

The outer line ran south along Granny White Pike to the hilly main salient south of the Acklen estate. This was the pivot point around which the Union armies marched against the Confederate left flank on Dec. 15, 1864.

The outer line then ran northwest to Bald Hill (currently Love Circle) where a strong battery was located. The line then turned north, with a short offset along the railroad, and then north to the river where Tennessee State University is now located.

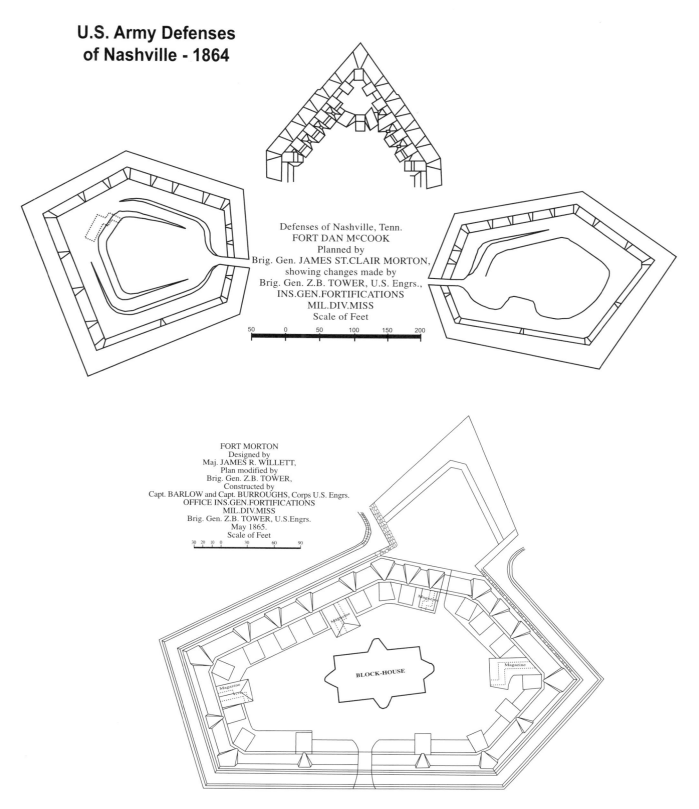

U.S. Army Defenses of Nashville - 1864

Defenses of Nashville, Tenn.
FORT DAN McCOOK
Planned by
Brig. Gen. JAMES ST.CLAIR MORTON,
showing changes made by
Brig. Gen. Z.B. TOWER, U.S. Engrs.,
INS.GEN.FORTIFICATIONS
MIL.DIV.MISS
Scale of Feet

50   0   50   100   150   200

FORT MORTON
Designed by
Maj. JAMES R. WILLETT,
Plan modified by
Brig. Gen. Z.B. TOWER,
Constructed by
Capt. BARLOW and Capt. BURROUGHS, Corps U.S. Engrs.
OFFICE INS.GEN.FORTIFICATIONS
MIL.DIV.MISS
Brig. Gen. Z.B. TOWER, U.S.Engrs.
May 1865.
Scale of Feet

30 20 10 0   30   60   90

Magazine

Magazine

Magazine

BLOCK-HOUSE

Magazine

*Drawings of fortifications adapted from The
Official Military Atlas of the Civil War*

Belmont Mansion

Belmont Mansion, an ornate Italianate villa built in 1850 outside the city limits of Nashville, was the home of Joseph and Adelicia Acklen.

Belmont was built on one of the highest hills in Nashville. Originally, the estate was known as Bellemonte, Italian for "beautiful mountain."

The mansion today is furnished in Victorian opulence with original and period pieces, gilded mirrors, marble statues from Europe, and oil paintings. During your guided tour you will learn about Belmont's mistress, Adelicia Acklen, who prevailed throughout the Civil War, three marriages, ten children, and the management of one of the largest fortunes in America.

An extraordinary character, Adelicia Acklen was one of the wealthiest women in the United States, with land holdings in Tennessee, Louisiana, and Texas.

At the time of the Civil War, the 180-acre estate included formal gardens with statuary and gazebos, a bear house, zoo, deer park, bowling alley, and art gallery. Many lavish formal balls were held in the mansion, usually on moonlit nights.

Joseph Acklen, who was Adelicia's second husband, was forced to flee to Louisiana when Union troops occupied Nashville in February 1862 and he never returned to Belmont.

During the war, Adelicia's husband died at their Louisiana plantation, and she was forced to travel there to preserve her property holdings. By plying the Union and Confederate authorities against each other, she was able to sell 2,000 bales of cotton to buyers in London. She traveled abroad after the war to collect her money and spent it on a shopping spree across Europe.

Although the mansion was located at the Union fortification line, it was not damaged during the Battle of Nashville in 1864. Union scouts used the 105-foot-tall brick water tower, which still exists, as a lookout point and to relay signals. The mansion served as the headquarters for Union Gen. T.J. Wood during the battle.

The mansion, the second largest antebellum house still standing, features the Grand Salon, the most elaborate domestic room in prewar Tennessee. It is furnished with Corinthian columns, chandeliers, and fine paintings and statuary. A lavish reception for 2,000 guests was conducted there following Adelicia's marriage to her third husband in 1867.

The mansion also features a grand staircase, the lavishly furnished tete-a-tete room, upstairs bedrooms, parlors, pantries with original china, the library, and the front hall with the marble statues of "Ruth Gleaning" and "Sleeping Children."

Belmont Mansion was named a National Historic Place in 1971 and opened to the public in 1976.

Belmont Mansion is located on the campus of Belmont University at 1900 Belmont Boulevard. The phone number is (615) 460-5459. Guided tours are available. Admission is charged; group rates are available. Hours are Mon.-Sat., 10-4 and Sun., 1-4 p.m. Closed major holidays. The website is www.belmontmansion.com.

⑮ Sunnyside

Sunnyside mansion is located inside Sevier Park on 12th Ave. South just north of the I-440 overpass. Sunnyside was located directly between the Union and Confederate lines prior to the Battle of Nashville on Dec. 15, 1864. Afterwards it served as a field hospital for wounded soldiers.

During renovation, bullet holes and cannon ball tracks found in the walls indicated that the house was heavily fired upon during the battle. Also found was the foundation of the oldest part of the home—a one-story log cabin built around 1820. Jesse Benton, the sister-in-law of statesman and artist Thomas Hart Benton, lived here before the Civil War.

⑯ Battle of Nashville Monument

The Battle of Nashville Monument (also called the Peace Monument) is one of the very few monuments dedicated to the soldiers of both sides of the Civil War. Dedicated on Armistice Day in 1927, the sculpture also memorializes the American soldiers who fought in France during World War I.

The monument park is located on Granny White Pike (12th Ave. South) between Battlefield Drive and Clifton Lane just south of the I-440 overpass (no access from I-440).

The memorial was designed by Italian sculptor Giuseppe Moretti on commission from the Ladies Battlefield Association. The bronze horses represent the North and the South which are yoked together by the youth, symbolizing all Americans who fought in the Civil War and World War I. "Unity" is inscribed on the banner with which he entwines the horses. The white granite obelisk topped with a marble angel stands 40 feet high.

Originally located on Franklin Pike at Thompson Lane (Site 19), the monument was severely damaged by storms in 1974 and virtually hidden from view by the construction of an interstate highway interchange. In 1999, a newly reconditioned monument was re-dedicated at the present site, which marks the center of the Confederate line on the first day of battle, Dec. 15, 1864.

(17) Redoubt No. 4

Confederate Redoubt No. 4 is located on Foster Hill Drive in the Green Hills residential section of the city. There is a marker placed by the Tennessee Historical Society.

On Dec. 10, 1864, Gen. Hood had ordered the construction of five redoubts (log and earth fortifications) near the Hillsboro Pike to protect his left flank. A winter storm froze the ground and the soldiers had not completed Redoubt No. 4 when the opening attack came on Dec. 15. U.S. troops formed along the ridge one half-mile to the west (now Estes Rd.). Two dozen cannons dueled with the four cannons in Redoubt No. 4 manned by 48 artillerymen of Lumden's Battery, supported by 148 men of the 29th Alabama infantry. Seven thousand U.S. infantrymen and dismounted cavalry began the assault at 2:15 p.m. The redoubt was captured about 3 p.m., with some prisoners taken. Ordered to hold this ground at all hazards, the greatly outnumbered Confederates had held out for about three hours under heavy fire. The U.S. forces continued east to fight the Confederates positioned behind a stone wall along Hillsboro Pike.

(18) Redoubt No. 1

Confederate Redoubt No. 1 is located at 3423 Benham Road on high ground and represents the northwest salient of the main Confederate line on the opening day of battle.

Redoubt No. 1 was one of five small forts built along the far left (west) flank of the main Confederate line. The forts were typically armed with a battery of four Napoleon artillery pieces, 85 artillerymen, and supported by 100 infantrymen.

On the first day of battle, the U.S. Army attacked all five forts. Redoubt No. 1 was the last to fall.

Today only the remnants of the earthworks remain. The site is owned and maintained by the Battle of Nashville Preservation Society.

(19) Old Monument Site

Still standing near Franklin Pike at Thompson Lane is the original stone base to the Battle of Nashville Peace Monument, dedicated in 1927. Refurbished and relocated in 1999, the monument is now located at Site No. 16.

What was once tranquil countryside is now a busy interstate highway intersection. And in 1974 a severe storm toppled the marble obelisk and angel.

During the first day of the battle, this ground was held by the Confederate forces of Gen. Stephen D. Lee in the center of the line.

The Battle of Nashville

The Battle of Nashville, fought Thursday and Friday, Dec. 15-16, 1864, was one of the most decisive—some say *the* most decisive—battles of the Civil War. The Union victory by Major General George H. Thomas virtually destroyed the Confederate Army of Tennessee, led by the bold and reckless Gen. John Bell Hood. The battle marked the end of major military action in the Western Theater. Four months later Lee surrendered to Grant in Virginia, and for all practical purposes the war was over.

The soldiers at Nashville hailed from 22 of the 34 states at the time. Missouri and Tennessee had soldiers in both armies. Fighting for the Union were men from Illinois, Indiana, Iowa, Kansas, Kentucky, Michigan, Minnesota, New York, Ohio, Pennsylvania, and Wisconsin.

Fighting for the South were men from Alabama, Arkansas, Florida, Georgia, Louisiana, Mississippi, North Carolina, South Carolina, and Texas.

Hood's Tennessee invasion of 1864

Following the fall of Atlanta, Ga. to Sherman in Sept. 1864, Hood moved northward to attack Sherman's supply lines. Sherman moved in pursuit but then decided to begin his famous March to the Sea, leaving Thomas behind at Nashville to protect his rear. Sherman left Atlanta on Nov. 15 and arrived in Savannah on the coast on Dec. 21.

Hood, meanwhile, formulated a bold—some might say desperate—plan to move north into Tennessee, attack and reclaim Nashville, and then perhaps deploy north of the Ohio River, capturing Chicago or Cincinnati. Another option was that he could march into Virginia to reinforce Gen. Robert E. Lee against Grant.

After waiting three long weeks in northern Alabama for supplies, Hood moved north into Tennessee on Nov. 22. His army comprised three corps under Lt. Gen. Alexander P. Stewart, Lt. Gen. Stephen D. Lee, and Major Gen. Benjamin F. Cheatham, with the cavalry commanded by Major Gen. Nathan Bedford Forrest.

At Columbia, Tenn., Hood outflanked Union Gen. John M. Schofield, who was racing north to the safety of the Nashville

Detail, Confederate Circle Monument, Mount Olivet Cemetery

fortifications. The anticipated envelopment of Schofield's army at Spring Hill did not materialize, and on Nov. 30 Hood attacked Schofield, who had entrenched at Franklin, in one of the bloodiest battles of the war. Six thousand Confederates were killed or wounded during the frontal assault, including 52 field-grade officers. Thirteen of the army's 28 general officers were killed, wounded, or missing. The next day, Schofield retreated to Nashville, leaving many of the soldiers in the weakened Army of Tennessee demoralized from the senseless slaughter.

Hood's army reaches Nashville

Hood reached the southern outskirts of Nashville on Dec. 2 and deployed an east-west line four miles long, much shorter than the seven miles of the Federal outer defenses around the city. Hood placed Stewart on the left flank, Lee in the center, and Cheatham on the right flank. On a north-south line on his left flank along the Hillsborough Pike, Hood began building five redoubts (small forts) to protect that

flank. Both Union and Confederate lines were anchored on bends in the Cumberland River.

From Dec. 2 until the battle itself, a regiment of 300 Southerners under Lt. Col. David C. Kelley, armed with four artillery pieces and stationed at Bell's Mills, six miles west of Nashville on the Cumberland River, fought six separate engagements with Union gunboats under Lt. Commander Leroy Fitch. River traffic was blocked by the Confederate gunners.

For the next two weeks, Hood's men waited for the inevitable Union attack, suffering greatly from exposure to the severe winter weather which began on Dec. 9. Many were shoeless and barely surviving on rations of parched corn. Hood made his headquarters at the home of John Overton, known as Travellers Rest.

Thomas prepares for battle

Meanwhile, Gen. Thomas was busy consolidating an assortment of troops and arguing with his superiors, who wanted him to attack Hood immediately. Back in Washington, U.S. Commander-in-Chief U.S. Grant noted, "There is no better man to repel an attack than Thomas but I fear he is too cautious to ever take the initiative."

Schofield's XXIII Corps (10,207 men) arrived in Nashville on Dec. 1 following the battle at Franklin. Also arriving was the IV Corps (14,171 men), now under command of Brig. Gen. Thomas J. Wood.

Major Gen. James B. Steedman's assortment of troops—convalescents, unattached units, and eight regiments of U.S. Colored Troops totaling 7,541 men—arrived by

Continued on Page 52

U.S. Regulars confront U.S. Volunteers in Smoky Row

A miniature Battle of Nashville erupted late in the evening of Nov. 25, 1864 in Smoky Row, a squalid part of town notorious for prostitution and hard drinking. Members of the 13th U.S. Infantry Regulars and volunteers of the 9th Pennsylvania and the 4th Michigan regiments argued over the relative merits of regular versus volunteer service. The altercation escalated into gunfire. The Regulars retreated to a house which was then attacked and taken over by the volunteers. At a second house, the Provost Marshal's men arrived in numbers sufficient to take everyone into custody, including 20 civilians who were kept in the guardhouse overnight. More than a hundred shots were fired during the melee. No one was injured, but one woman had her shoe shot off.

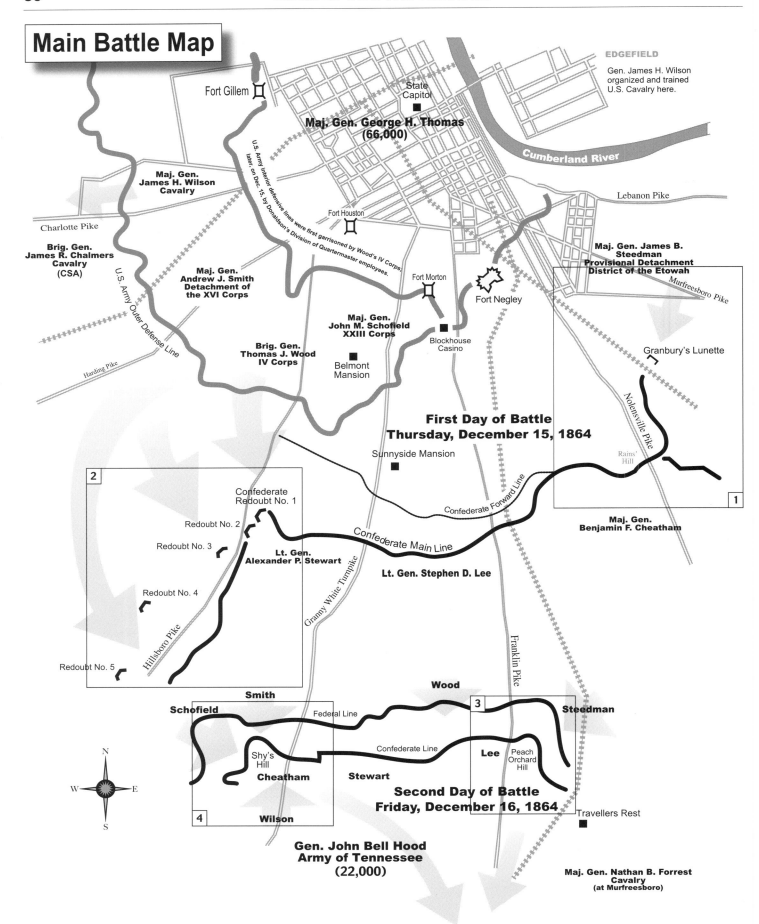

Main Battle Map

EDGEFIELD

Gen. James H. Wilson organized and trained U.S. Cavalry here.

Fort Gillem

State Capitol

Maj. Gen. George H. Thomas (66,000)

Cumberland River

Maj. Gen. James H. Wilson Cavalry

U.S. Army Interior defensive lines were first garrisoned by Wood's IV Corps; later, on Dec. 15, by Donaldson's Division of Quartermaster employees.

Charlotte Pike

Fort Houston

Lebanon Pike

Brig. Gen. James R. Chalmers Cavalry (CSA)

Maj. Gen. James B. Steedman Provisional Detachment District of the Etowah

Maj. Gen. Andrew J. Smith Detachment of the XVI Corps

Fort Morton

Fort Negley

Murfreesboro Pike

U.S. Army Outer Defense Line

Harding Pike

Maj. Gen. John M. Schofield XXIII Corps

Blockhouse Casino

Granbury's Lunette

Brig. Gen. Thomas J. Wood IV Corps

Belmont Mansion

Nolensville Pike

Rains' Hill

First Day of Battle Thursday, December 15, 1864

Sunnyside Mansion

2

Confederate Redoubt No. 1

Confederate Forward Line

1

Redoubt No. 2

Maj. Gen. Benjamin F. Cheatham

Redoubt No. 3

Confederate Main Line

Redoubt No. 4

Lt. Gen. Alexander P. Stewart

Lt. Gen. Stephen D. Lee

Granny White Turnpike

Redoubt No. 5

Hillsboro Pike

Franklin Pike

Smith

Wood

Schofield

Steedman

3

Federal Line

Confederate Line

Lee

Peach Orchard Hill

Shy's Hill

Cheatham

Stewart

Second Day of Battle Friday, December 16, 1864

N
W   E
S

4

Wilson

Travellers Rest

Gen. John Bell Hood Army of Tennessee (22,000)

Maj. Gen. Nathan B. Forrest Cavalry (at Murfreesboro)

Special Field Order 342
Issued Dec. 14, 1864 by Gen. George H. Thomas, Commanding

As soon as the state of the weather will admit of offensive operations the troops will move against the enemy's position in the following order:

Maj. Gen. A. J. Smith, commanding Detachment of the Army of the Tennessee, after forming his troops on and near the Hardin pike, in front of his present position, will make a vigorous assault on the enemy's left.

Major-General Wilson, commanding the Cavalry Corps, Military Division of the Mississippi, with three divisions, will move on and support General Smith's right, assisting, as far as possible, in carrying the left of the enemy's position, and be in readiness to throw his force upon the enemy the moment a favorable opportunity occurs. Major-General Wilson will also send one division on the Charlotte pike to clear that road of the enemy and observe in the direction of Bell's Landing, to protect our right rear until the enemy's position is fairly turned, when it will rejoin the main force.

Brig. Gen. T. J. Wood, commanding the Fourth Army Corps, after leaving a strong skirmish line in his works from Laurens' Hill to his extreme right, will form the remainder of the Fourth Corps on the Hillsborough pike, to support General Smith's left, and operate on the left and rear of the enemy's advanced position on the Montgomery Hill.

Major-General Schofield, commanding Twenty-third Army Corps, will replace Brigadier-General Kimball's division, of the Fourth Corps, with his troops, and occupy the trenches from Fort Negley to Laurens' Hill with a strong skirmish line. He will move with the remainder of his force in front of the works and co-operate with General Wood, protecting the latter's left flank against an attack by the enemy.

Major-General Steedman, commanding District of the Etowah, will occupy the interior line in rear of his present position, stretching from the reservoir on the Cumberland River to Fort Negley, with a strong skirmish line, and mass the remainder of his force in its present position, to act according to the exigencies which may arise during these operations.

Brigadier-General Miller, with the troops forming the garrison of Nashville, will occupy the interior line from the battery on Hill 210 to the extreme right, including the inclosed work on the Hyde's Ferry road.

The quartermaster's troops, under command of Brigadier-General Donaldson, will, if necessary, be posted on the interior line from Fort Morton to the battery on Hill 210. The troops occupying the interior line will be under the direction of Major-General Steedman, who is charged with the immediate defense of Nashville during the operations around the city.

Should the weather permit the troops will be formed [in time] to commence operations at 6 a.m. on the 15th, or as soon thereafter as practicable.

Official Records, The War of the Rebellion, Vol. XLV, Pt. II, 183-84.

(Library of Congress)

The Union inner defensive works around Nashville were quiet during the battle.

Forrest and Bate deployed to Murfreesboro

Upon his arrival at Nashville, Gen. Hood deployed the division of Major Gen. William B. Bate and 1,600 men to attack the garrison at Murfreesboro, 28 miles to the southeast.

Bate wisely did not attack the garrison at Fortress Rosecrans, which numbered 8,000 Union troops under Major Gen. Lovell Rousseau. Gen. Nathan B. Forrest's cavalry was also dispatched to Murfreesboro, destroying railroad tracks along the way. Forrest took overall command and managed to entice a column of Union infantry out of the fort, commanded by Major Gen. Robert H. Milroy. On Dec. 7, in what was called the Battle of the Cedars, Milroy routed the Confederates and returned to the fort the next day. Bate returned to Nashville on Dec. 9 and Forrest continued to destroy the railroad, not returning to the Army of Tennessee until after the Battle of Nashville. Historians consider Hood's deployment of Forrest, the South's best cavalry commander, to Murfreesboro as a major tactical blunder.

Continued from Page 49
rail from Chattanooga. His corps was called the Provisional Detachment of the District of the Etowah. Commanding the 7th Indiana was Col. Benjamin Harrison, who would later become the nation's 23rd President (1889-93).

On Dec. 1, the XVI Corps, frontier troops under Major Gen. Andrew J. Smith totaling 10,461 men, arrived from Missouri in a 59-boat convoy. The normally restrained Thomas was so glad to see Smith he gave him a hearty bear hug.

In addition to waiting for the troops to arrive, Thomas also had to bolster his cavalry and wait out the inclement winter weather. Major Gen. James H. Wilson was put in charge of the cavalry and managed to assemble a formidable force of 12,000 troopers, all armed with the new seven-shot Spencer repeating rifle. The sleet and ice storm of Dec. 9 made operations untenable for several days, infuriating the anxious Grant. Federal authorities were so nervous about Hood's threat against Nashville that Grant threatened to replace Thomas with Schofield, then changed his mind, then prepared to travel by rail to Nashville himself. On Dec. 14th the cold weather lifted, and Thomas issued his Special Field Order 342—plans for the attack on the 15th.

The defenders would attack

Steedman would strike the Confederate right flank in the eastern sector as a feint, or secondary attack, forcing Hood to send reinforcements from his left flank. Wood would hold the center while Smith and Wilson would swing around in a giant pivoting movement and attack Hood's left flank in force. Initially assigned as a reserve, Schofield asked for and received approval to participate in the attack.

The defenses around Nashville would be held by Post Commander Gen. John F. Miller's men and by the employees of Quartermaster James L. Donaldson.

All in all, Hood with 22,000 men was outnumbered three-to-one by Thomas with about 66,000. In addition, thousands of Nashvillians watched the two-day battle from hilltops and rooftops. "No army on the continent ever played on any field to so large and so sullen an audience," according to one Union officer.

The first day of battle begins

On the morning of Thurs., Dec. 15, a heavy ground-hugging fog delayed the movement of U.S. troops and screened them from Confederate eyes. The big seige guns of Fort Negley and the other Union batteries opened fire against the Confederate lines.

At 8:00 a.m. Steedman's troops advanced

Continued on Page 55

Forrest's destructive raid on Johnsonville depot too late

After the fall of Atlanta, Ga. in Sept. 1864, Hood ordered Confederate Gen. Nathan Bedford Forrest to attack Sherman's supply lines in Tennessee in an attempt to force Sherman to retreat. On Nov. 4, cavalry under Forrest deployed 12 pieces of artillery on the west bank of the Tennessee River opposite the huge Union supply depot at Johnsonville. During 1864, supplies from the North had been transported to the depot by river, offloaded and stored at Johnsonville, and then hauled 78 miles east to Nashville on the Nashville and Northwestern Railroad.

At 2 p.m., the Confederate guns fired upon the transports, barges, and gunboats at the depot and then bombarded the depot itself. The Union commander, Col. C.R. Thompson, erroneously thinking Forrest would cross the river and capture the garrison, ordered the rest of the Union supplies destroyed. The raid destroyed four gunboats, 14 transports, 17 barges, 33 pieces of artillery, and approximately 100,000 tons of quartermaster stores. One hundred and fifty Union men were captured. Forrest suffered two men killed and nine wounded. The loss of Federal property was estimated at $2 million to $6 million. The raid, however, had little consequence as Sherman had already received enough supplies for his March to the Sea.

On Nov. 18, Forrest reported to Hood in northern Alabama, and four days later Hood moved north into Tennessee.

BATTLE OF NASHVILLE BATTLE MAP

1 **First Day - Dec. 15th, 1864 - East Sector**
Diversionary Attack Against CSA Right Flank

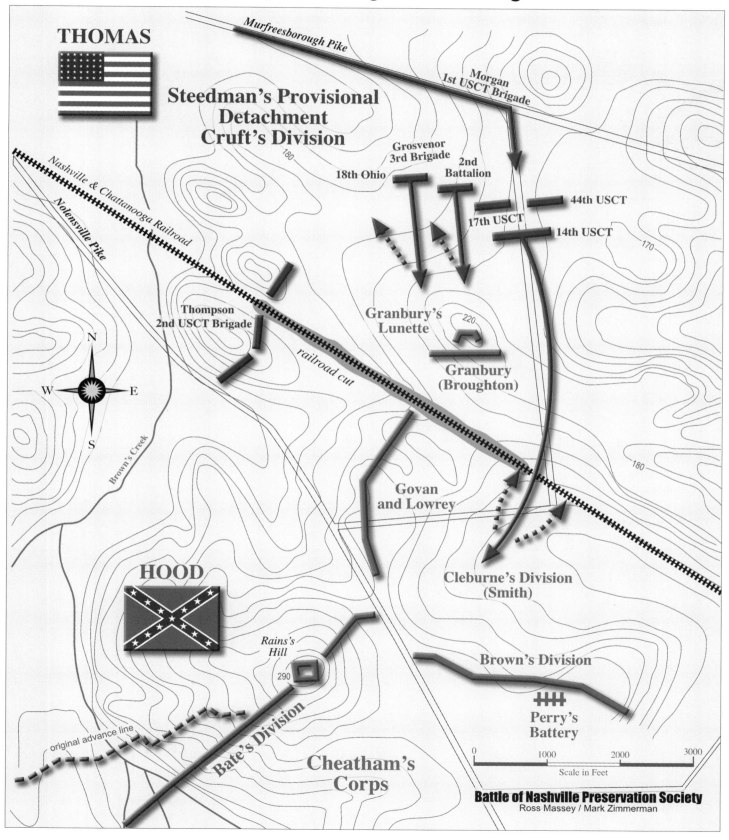

THOMAS

Murfreesborough Pike

Morgan
1st USCT Brigade

Steedman's Provisional
Detachment
Cruft's Division

180

Grosvenor
3rd Brigade

2nd
Battalion

18th Ohio

44th USCT

17th USCT

14th USCT

170

Nashville & Chattanooga Railroad

Nolensville Pike

Thompson
2nd USCT Brigade

railroad cut

Granbury's
Lunette

220

Granbury
(Broughton)

180

N
W   E
S

Brown's Creek

Govan
and Lowrey

Cleburne's Division
(Smith)

HOOD

Rains's
Hill

Brown's Division

290

Perry's
Battery

Bate's Division

original advance line

Cheatham's
Corps

0   1000   2000   3000
Scale in Feet

Battle of Nashville Preservation Society
Ross Massey / Mark Zimmerman

BATTLE OF NASHVILLE BATTLE MAP

2　First Day - Dec. 15th, 1864 - West Sector
Main Attack Against CSA Redoubts on Left Flank

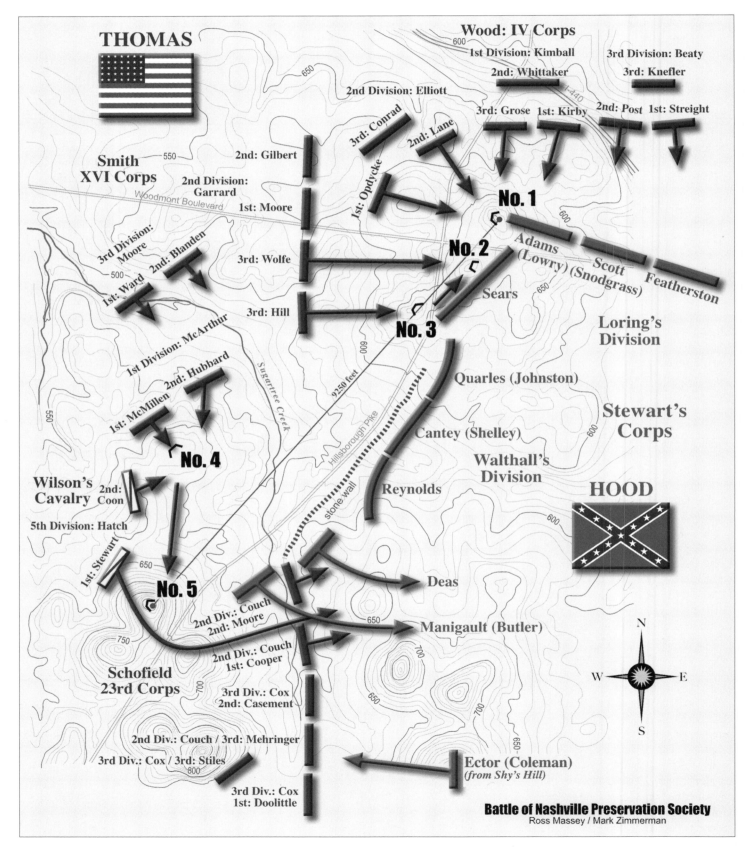

Continued from Page 52

against the Confederate right flank held by Cheatham. Four regiments of U.S. Colored Troops under Col. Charles R. Thompson moved against and occupied some abandoned Confederate earthworks and remained there the rest of the day. The brigade of Lt. Col. Charles Grosvenor attacked but was easily repulsed. The three USCT regiments of Col. Thomas J. Morgan rounded the right flank and moved toward the rear of the Confederate troops, not realizing that the end of the line was actually a lunette manned by Granbury's brigade of Texans under Capt. E.T. Broughton. Caught in a crossfire, the U.S. troops suffered heavy casualties, some men jumping into a steep railroad cut where they were mowed down.

Despite Steedman's attack on the right flank, Hood correctly perceived the main attack as coming on his left. Subsequently, during the remainder of the day he moved portions of Lee's corps from the center to the left flank, including the division of Major Gen. Edward Johnson (brigades of Manigault, Deas, Brantley, and Sharp). Most of these reinforcements reached the left flank too late to have an effect.

At 10 a.m., the grand movement began against the Confederate left flank, held by Stewart. Wilson's cavalry and Smith's infantry marched out of the defensive fortifications and wheeled first westward and then southward. In the process, the Confederate cavalry brigade of Col. Edmund Rucker fell back to the Bell's Bend area and Ector's infantry brigade under Col. David Coleman fell back to the extreme Confederate left flank which ran south along the Hillsborough Pike.

U.S. cavalry under Brig. Gen. Edward Hatch advanced to the Belle Meade plantation in the southwest sector, where they captured and burned the supply wagons of Brig. Gen. James Chalmers. Later in the day, Confederate cavalry under Lt. James Dinkins tried to retrieve the wagons and charged into a brisk skirmish with Union infantry on the front lawn of the estate.

At 12:30 p.m., Wood's corps began their movement out of the defense lines. The brigade of Col. Sidney Post of Brig. Gen. Samuel Beatty's Third Division charged up and captured Montgomery Hill near the salient of the Confederate left flank. Unknown to Post at the time, the Confederates had abandoned this formidable position several days earlier.

Redoubt No. 4 came under artillery fire from Col. William McMillen's brigade (Brig. Gen. John McArthur's Division of Smith's XVI Corps) to the west. Bravely holding out there for three hours against overwhelming numbers were the 48 artillerymen of Capt. Charles Lumsden and the 100 men of the 29th Alabama. The fort was abandoned only after the artilleryman with the friction primers had run off.

The U.S. cavalry of Col. Datus E. Coon of Hatch's Division reached Redoubt No. 5, the southernmost small fort along the Hillsborough Pike. After an artillery duel of about an hour, Coon, along with Col. McMillen's brigade, overpowered the defenders of the two-howitzer battery in the fort.

Against orders to stay put, Col. Sylvester G. Hill of McArthur's Division charged his brigade up the hill to Redoubt No. 3 and captured it. As he ordered his men to assault Redoubt No. 2, a bullet struck him in the forehead, killing him instantly. When 200 of his men attacked the redoubt, the defenders fled.

Now, at 4 p.m., the entire Confederate west flank was under heavy assault from three directions. Needed reinforcements from the right flank had yet to arrive. Taking the brunt of the assault along the pike was the division of Major Gen. Edward C. Walthall.

Positioned at the salient near Redoubt No. 1 were the troops of Major Gen. William W. Loring. Steadily advancing against them was Wood's IV Corps. Redoubt No. 1, the last fort to fall, was easily captured by Union skirmishers.

Confederates fall back to new line

Outnumbered, surrounded on three sides, and bombarded by artillery, Stewart's corps cut a hasty retreat to their east and south. The saving grace of the Army of Tennessee that day was the coming of darkness at about 6 p.m.

Hood's men drew back to a much shorter east-west line of about 2.5 miles extending from Compton's Hill (later named Shy's Hill in honor of Confederate Col. William Shy, who was killed defending it) on the west flank to Peach Orchard Hill or Overton Hill on the east flank. On the second day of battle, Cheatham was deployed on the left flank on Shy's Hill, Stewart in the center along a stone wall, and Lee on the right flank at Peach Orchard Hill.

The second day of battle

At 8:30 a.m. on Dec. 16, Smith's XVI Corps moved to within 600 yards of Shy's Hill and began to bombard the small prominence with artillery shells. To the west of the hill, Schofield was apprehensive of a counter-attack by Hood and asked for reinforcements. To the south of the hill, Wilson's cavalry was ordered by Schofield to stand in place. An opportunity to cut off Granny White Pike, Hood's avenue of escape (in addition to the Franklin Pike), was thus lost. By noon, rain began falling.

Steedman and Wood spent the entire morning moving into position north and east of Peach Orchard Hill on the right flank. At 2:45 p.m., four U.S. brigades moved against the hill, which was held by Lee's corps. The men of Col. Abel Streight and Col. Sidney Post took heavy fire and were slowed by abatis (felled trees) and other obstructions. Post was wounded in the leg and his attack faltered. A similar fate befell the U.S. Colored Troops of Col. Thompson, who then scattered. But one regiment, the 13th USCT, advanced to the parapets of Peach Orchard Hill. Five colorbearers, one after the other, were shot down at the parapet. "They came only to die," wrote one Union officer after the battle. Confederate Brig. Gen. James Holtzclaw of Clayton's Division was so impressed by the bravery of the black troops that he cited them in his official report, which was very uncommon. The 13th USCT regiment lost 220 men. The Union attacking forces suffered 1,000 casualties.

Over on the west flank, at 2:00 p.m., Gen. McArthur of the XVI Corps was determined to take Shy's Hill from the north. He concluded that the Confederates had dug in too far on top of the hill and their artillery and rifles could not properly target men coming up the hill. At 4:00 p.m., without orders, he commanded McMillen's brigade to take the hill, backed by the brigades of Col. Lucius Hubbard and Col. William Marshall.

Thomas had been urging the reluctant Schofield to advance his men when they saw McArthur's charge up the hill to their
Continued on Page 58

BATTLE OF NASHVILLE BATTLE MAP

3 Second Day - Dec. 16th, 1864 - East Sector Secondary Attack Against Peach Orchard Hill

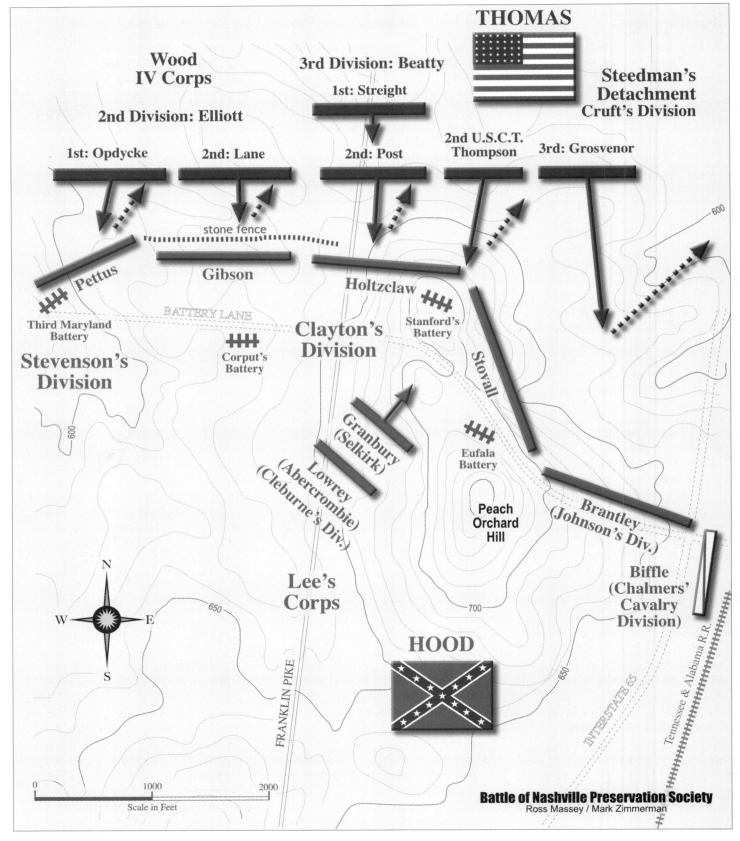

BATTLE OF NASHVILLE BATTLE MAP

4 **Second Day - Dec. 16th, 1864 - West Sector**
Union Main Attack Against Shy's Hill (Compton Hill)

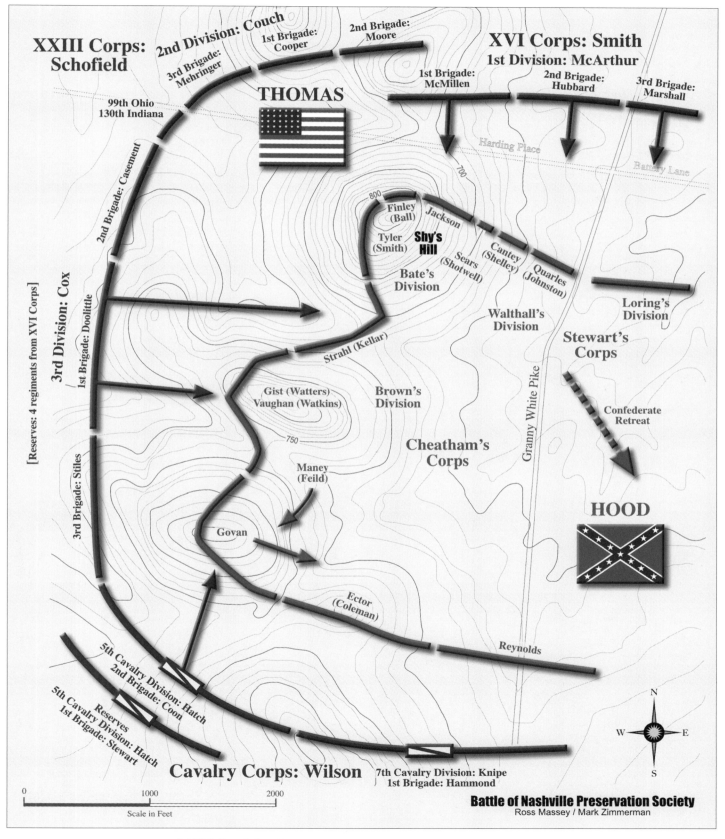

Continued from Page 55
left. Thomas then calmly ordered Schofield to do the same.

Hood believed that Shy's Hill was impregnable and had moved Ector's brigade and the brigade of Brig. Gen. Daniel Reynolds off the hill. Now, after hours of being bombarded by artillery from three sides, Major Gen. William Bate's Division of Cheatham's Corps faced overwhelming numbers in their front. The hardest hit were Tyler's Brigade under Brig. Gen. Thomas Benton Smith and Finley's Brigade under Major Glover Ball. Furious hand-to-hand fighting broke out and the Confederate ranks broke. Col. Shy was shot in the forehead at point-blank range. Like wildfire, panic spread among the Southerners, who remembered the slaughter at Franklin and now faced overwhelming numbers on three sides with no chance of reinforcements. Men threw down their weapons and ran to the rear. "I have never seen an army so confused and demoralized," said one Confederate officer. Efforts by the officers to stem the tide proved

futile.

The U.S. Army at Shy's Hill captured 1,533 men, 85 officers, and eight cannons. Twenty-five-year-old Brig. Gen. Thomas Benton Smith was captured on Shy's Hill. As he was being led to the rear he was attacked by Col. McMillen, who struck him on the head three times with his saber, opening his skull. Although the wound was thought to be fatal, Smith survived until 1923 but spent most of those postwar years in an insane asylum.

The long retreat begins

The Army of Tennessee fled south down the Franklin Pike towards Brentwood while U.S. cavalry moved down the Granny White Pike to cut them off. Lee's Corps on the right flank formed a protective rear guard on the Franklin Pike. Confederate cavalry under Col. Edmund Rucker erected a barricade across Granny White Pike and engaged Wilson's pursuing troopers in a spirited fight which allowed the retreating Confederates to escape into the night. Rucker and Col.

George Spalding of the 12th Tenn. (US) Cavalry fought a mounted saber duel until Rucker was shot in the arm by an infantryman and captured.

The day after the battle the headlines in the Nashville newspapers proclaimed "Hood's army demoralized and in full retreat" and "The Rebels completely routed. They flee in a perfect panic."

"Hood's army has endured fatigues and privations almost beyond belief," remarked an agent of the U.S. Christian Commission, a support organization for the U.S. troops.

All the churches in Nashville, along with the courthouse, were filled with 2,000 wounded soldiers, soon joined by 3,800 wounded earlier at the battle at Franklin.

Details were sent out to clean up the immense battlefield the weekend after the battle. It took four days to bury the dead and collect all the discarded weapons.

Thus began for the Confederates a grueling 10-day, 100-mile retreat in the cold rain. On Dec. 17, Gen. Lee was wounded and command of the rear guard passed to Major Gen. Carter L. Stevenson. On Dec. 19, Forrest rejoined the army at Columbia and his men took over as the rear guard, engaging Wilson's troopers in several desperate holding actions.

On Dec. 26, Hood's army began crossing the Tennessee River in northern Alabama on a pontoon bridge. Union gunboats delayed and lost the opportunity to shell the troops.

Aftermath of battle

In January 1865, Hood resigned as commander of the army. Many soldiers in the Army of Tennessee went to North Carolina to fight under Gen. Joseph Johnston, who surrendered to Sherman on April 26.

As a major Civil War battle, Nashville did not produce a relatively large number of casualties. Thomas listed his casualties at 3,061—387 killed, 2,562 wounded, and 112 missing. A third of the casualties were suffered at Overton Hill on the second day of battle. Thomas said he also captured 4,462 prisoners and 53 pieces of artillery.

The Army of Tennessee lost an estimated 2,300 men killed or wounded. Three generals were captured—Edward Johnson, H.R. Jackson, and Thomas B. Smith.

During Hood's entire 1864 Tennessee campaign it is estimated that he lost 23,500 of his 38,000 men.

The Battle of Nashville Peace Monument pays homage to the fighting men of both sides of the war.

Battle of Nashville Order of Battle • U.S. Army
Maj. Gen. George H. Thomas, Commanding

Major General George Henry Thomas (1816-70)
A native Virginian, he was disowned by his family for remaining loyal to the Union. He graduated West Point in 1840, ranked 12th in the class. He served in the artillery during the Seminole and Mexican wars. He served in the 2nd Cavalry under Albert Sidney Johnston and Robert E. Lee. In the Civil War, he commanded troops defeating Confederates under Zollicoffer at Fishing Creek, Ky. in Jan. 1862. He was known as the "Rock of Chickamauga" for standing firm at that battle in Sept. 1863 while the rest of Rosecrans' Union army was routed. His men from the Army of the Cumberland stormed Missionary Ridge without orders and broke the seige of Chattanooga in Nov. 1863. His army was the central force in Sherman's campaign against Atlanta, May-Sept. 1864. Following the victory at Nashville, Thomas was promoted to Major General, U.S. Army, and received the "Thanks of Congress." He served in the Army until his death in California. He is buried at Oakwood Cemetery, Troy, NY.

XVI Corps or Detachment Army of the Tennessee: Maj. Gen. Andrew J. Smith

Major Gen. Andrew Jackson Smith (1815-97)
Born in Pennsylvania, he graduated from West Point in 1838 and served with the Dragoons (cavalry) in the West for 23 years. His troops served with Sherman at Chickasaw Bluffs and Vicksburg, Miss., and in the Red River campaigns. He defeated Forrest at Tupelo on July 14, 1864. His rugged troops were assigned to so many different locales that they became known as the "lost tribes of Israel" and "Smith's guerillas." After the war he served as postmaster and city auditor of St. Louis, Mo. He is buried at Bellefontaine Cemetery, St. Louis.

First Division: Brig. Gen. John McArthur

1st Brigade: Col. William L. McMillen
114th Illinois; 93rd Indiana; 10th Minnesota

2nd Brigade: Col. Lucius F. Hubbard
5th, 9th Minnesota; 11th Missouri; 8th Wisconsin;
2nd Battery Iowa Light Artillery (Reed)

3rd Brigade: Col. Sylvester G. Hill (k), Col. William R. Marshall
12th, 35th Iowa; 7th Minnesota; 33rd Missouri;
Battery I 2nd Missouri Light Artillery (Julian)

Second Division: Brig. Gen. Kenner Garrard

1st Brigade: Col. David Moore
119th, 122nd Illinois; 89th Indiana; 21st Missouri;
9th Battery Indiana Light Artillery (Calfee)

2nd Brigade: Col. James L. Gilbert
58th Illinois; 27th, 32nd Iowa; 10th Kansas;
3rd Battery Indiana Light Artillery (Ginn)

3rd Brigade: Col. Edward H. Wolfe
49th, 117th Illinois; 52nd Indiana; 178th New York;
Battery G, 2nd Illinois Light Artillery (Lowell)

Third Division: Col. Jonathan B. Moore

1st Brigade: Col. Lyman M. Ward
72nd Illinois; 40th Missouri; 14th, 33rd Wisconsin

2nd Brigade: Col. Leander Blanden
81st, 95th Illinois; 44th Missouri Artillery;
11th Battery Indiana Light Artillery (Morse);
Battery A, 2nd Missouri Light Artillery (Zepp)

IV Army Corps: Brig. Gen. Thomas J. Wood

Brig. Gen. Thomas John Wood (1823-1906)
Born in Kentucky, he graduated West Point in 1845 and won honors in the Mexican War. He saw action at Shiloh under Buell; at Perryville, Ky.; and at Murfreesboro, TN, where he was wounded. In a controversial incident at Chickamauga in Sept. 1863 he moved his division under orders and opened a gap in the Union lines which allowed Longstreet to rout the Union right wing. His men were first to crest Missionary Ridge at Chattanooga in Nov. 1863. He was again wounded at Lovejoy Station, Sept. 1864. In 1865 he was promoted to Major General and retired in 1868. He died in Dayton, Ohio. He is buried at West Point, NY.

First Division: Brig. Gen. Nathan Kimball

1st Brigade: Col. Isaac M. Kirby
21st, 38th Illinois; 31st, 81st Indiana; 90th Ohio

2nd Brigade: Brig. Gen. Walter C. Whittaker
96th, 115th Illinois; 35th Indiana; 21st, 23rd Kentucky; 45th, 51st Ohio

3rd Brigade: Brig. Gen. William Grose
75th, 80th, 84th Illinois; 9th, 30th, 36th, 84th Indiana; 77th Pennsylvania

Second Division: Brig. Gen. Washington L. Elliott

1st Brigade: Col. Emerson Opdycke
36th, 44th, 73rd, 74th, 88th Illinois; 125th Ohio; 24th Wisconsin

2nd Brigade: Col. John Q. Lane
100th Illinois; 40th, 57th Indiana; 28th Kentucky; 26th, 97th Ohio

3rd Brigade: Col. Joseph Conrad
42nd, 51st, 79th Illinois; 15th Missouri; 64th, 65th Ohio

Third Division: Brig. Gen. Samuel Beatty

1st Brigade: Col. Abel D. Streight
89th Illinois; 51st Indiana; 8th Kansas; 15th, 49th Ohio

2nd Brigade: Col. P. Sidney Post (w)
59th Illinois; 41st, 71st, 93rd, 124th Ohio

3rd Brigade: Col. Frederick Knefler
79th, 86th Indiana; 13th, 19th Ohio

Artillery: Maj. Wilbur F. Goodspeed
Light Batteries: 25th Indiana (Sturm); 1st Kentucky (Thomason);
1st Michigan (De Vries); 1st Ohio G (Marshall); 6th Ohio (Baldwin);
Battery B, Pennsylvania Light Artillery (Ziegler);
Battery M, 4th U.S. (Canby)

Battle of Nashville Order of Battle • U.S. Army
Maj. Gen. George H. Thomas, Commanding

XXIII Army Corps: Maj. Gen. John M. Schofield

Major Gen. John McAllister Schofield (1831-1906)

Born in New York and raised in the Midwest, he graduated from West Point in 1853, ranking 7th in the class. He commanded militia and the Army of the Frontier in Missouri from 1861-63. He led the XXIII Corps during Sherman's Atlanta campaign and inflicted heavy losses on Hood's army at the Battle of Franklin, Nov. 30, 1864. After the war he served as Secretary of War under President Johnson, West Point superintendent (1876-81), and commander of the U.S. Army in 1888-95. He recommended that Pearl Harbor be acquired as a naval base. He is buried at Arlington National Cemetery.

Second Division: Maj. Gen. Darius N. Couch
1st Brigade: Brig. Gen. Joseph A. Cooper 130th Indiana; 26th Kentucky; 25th Michigan; 99th Ohio; 3rd, 6th Tennessee
2nd Brigade: Col. Orlando H. Moore 107th Illinois; 80th, 129th Indiana; 23rd Michigan; 111th, 118th Ohio
3rd Brigade: Col. John Mehringer 91st, 123rd Indiana; 50th, 183rd Ohio
Artillery: Light Batteries: 13th Indiana (Harvey); 19th Ohio (Wilson)

Third Division: Brig. Gen. Jacob D. Cox
1st Brigade: Col. Charles C. Doolittle 12th, 16th Kentucky; 100th, 104th Ohio; 8th Tennessee
2nd Brigade: Col. John S. Casement 65th Illinois; 65th, 124th Indiana; 103rd Ohio; 5th Tennessee
3rd Brigade: Col. Israel N. Stiles 112th Illinois; 63rd, 120th, 128th Indiana
Artillery: Light Batteries: 23rd Indiana (Wilber); Battery D, 1st Ohio (Cockerill)

Provisional Detachment, District of the Etowah: Maj. Gen. James B. Steedman

Major Gen. James Blair Steedman (1817-83)

A Pennsylvanian, he was a civilian general who had little formal education and had worked as a printer, Ohio legislator, and owner of the *Toledo Times* newspaper. Active in Democratic Party politics. His men served at Perryville, Ky.; Murfreesboro, Tenn.; and at Chickamauga, where he led an attack carrying the regimental colors after his horse was shot from under him. He commanded the Post of Chattanooga from Oct. 1863 to May 1864. After the war he collected revenues in New Orleans, and then edited a paper in Toledo and served as chief of police there. He is buried at Woodlawn Cemetery, Toledo, Ohio.

Provisional Division: Brig. Gen. Charles Cruft
1st Colored Brigade: Col. Thomas J. Morgan 14th, 16th, 17th, 18th, 44th U.S. Colored Troops
2nd Colored Brigade: Col. Charles R. Thompson 12th, 13th, 100th U.S. Colored Troops; 1st Battery Kansas Light Artillery (Tennessee)
1st Brigade: Col. Benjamin Harrison 3 battalions from 20th Army Corps
2nd Brigade: Col. John C. Mitchell men from detached duty Army of the Tennessee
3rd Brigade: Lt. Col. Charles H. Grosvenor 68th Indiana; 18th, 121st Ohio; 2nd Battalion 14th Army Corps
Artillery: 20th Battery Indiana Light Artillery (Osborne); 18th Battery Ohio Light Artillery (Aleshire)

Post of Nashville: Brig. Gen. John F. Miller

Brig. Gen. John Franklin Miller (1831-86)

Born in Indiana, he was a lawyer and state senator. As a colonel, he commanded the 29th Indiana regiment at Shiloh, Corinth, and in Kentucky. He commanded a brigade at Murfreesboro under Negley, and was wounded at Liberty Gap, Tenn. in June 1863. He was assigned Post Commander of Nashville in May 1864 and commanded 12 infantry regiments and 14 batteries at the city's defenses during the Battle of Nashville. Resigning in 1865, he worked in the fur trade in California and served as U.S. Senator of that state until his death. He is buried at Arlington National Cemetery.

Brigade: (20th Army Corps, 4th Division, 2nd Brigade) Col. Edwin C. Mason 142nd Indiana; 45th New York; 176th, 179th, 182nd Ohio
Unattached: 3rd Kentucky; 28th Michigan; 173rd Ohio; 78th Pennsylvania; Veteran Reserve Corps; 44th, 45th Wisconsin
Garrison Artillery: Light Batteries: Bridge's Illinois (White); 2nd (Whicher); 4th (Johnson); 12th (White); 21st (Andrew); 22nd (Nicholson); 24th (Allen) Indiana Batteries; Battery F, 1st Michigan (Paddock); Batteries A (Scovill), E (Reckard) 1st Ohio; 20th Ohio Battery (Backus); Batteries C (Grisby), D (Leinert), 1st Tennessee; Battery A, 2nd U.S. Colored (Meigs)

Battle of Nashville Order of Battle • U.S. Army
Maj. Gen. George H. Thomas, Commanding

Cavalry Corps: Maj. Gen. James H. Wilson

Major Gen. James Harrison Wilson (1837-1925)
Born in Illinois, he graduated West Point in 1860, sixth in his class. He was a topographical engineer and an aide to McClellan and Grant. He was inspector general of the Army of the Tennessee during the Vicksburg campaign. In Oct. 1863 he was promoted to brigadier general of volunteer infantry. After Chattanooga and Knoxville, he was named chief of the cavalry bureau in Washington. He commanded a division of Sheridan's cavalry in Virginia and in Oct. 1864 he became chief of cavalry of Sherman's Military Division of the Mississippi. In 1865 he led one of the war's most successful cavalry raids into Alabama and Georgia, defeating Forrest in the process. Retiring in 1870, he managed railroads, traveled, and wrote on a variety of topics. At the age of 61, he volunteered and fought in the Spanish-American War in Puerto Rico and Cuba and in the Boxer Rebellion in China. He is buried at Old Swedes Churchyard, Wilmington, N.C.

First Division: Brig. Gen. Edward M. McCook

1st Brigade: Brig. Gen. John T. Croxton
8th Iowa; 4th Kentucky Mounted Infantry; 2nd Michigan; 1st Tennessee;
Board of Trade Battery, Illinois Light Artillery (Robinson)

2nd Brigade: Col. Oscar H. La Grange
Detached in pursuit of Lyon's raid into western Kentucky

3rd Brigade: Bvt. Brig. Gen. Louis D. Watkins
Detached in pursuit of Lyon's raid into western Kentucky

Fifth Division: Brig. Gen. Edward Hatch

1st Brigade: Col. Robert R. Stewart
3rd Illinois; 11th Indiana; 12th Missouri; 10th Tennessee

2nd Brigade: Col. Datus E. Coon
6th, 7th, 9th Illinois; 2nd Iowa; 12th Tennessee;
Battery I, 1st Illinois Light Artillery (McCartney)

Sixth Division: Brig. Gen. Richard W. Johnson

1st Brigade: Col. Thomas J. Harrison
16th Illinois; 5th Iowa; 7th Ohio

2nd Brigade: Col. James Biddle
14th Illinois; 6th Indiana; 8th Michigan; 3rd Tennessee
Artillery: Battery I, 4th U.S. (Frank G. Smith)

Seventh Division: Brig. Gen. Joseph F. Knipe

1st Brigade: Bvt. Brig. Gen. John H. Hammond
9th, 10th Indiana; 19th Pennsylvania; 2nd, 4th Tennessee

2nd Brigade: Col. Gilbert M.L. Johnson
12th, 13th Indiana; 8th Tennessee Artillery;
14th Battery Ohio Light Artillery (Myers)

Quartermaster's Division: Bvt. Brig. Gen. James L. Donaldson

Brevet Brig. Gen. James Lowry Donaldson (1814-85)

Native of Maryland and 1836 graduate of West Point, he served in the Seminole and Mexican wars. He was chief quartermaster of New Mexico before the war. He was Chief Quartermaster for the Department of the Cumberland, Nov. 1863 to June 1865, stationed in Nashville.

Brig. Gen. Zealous Bates Tower (1819-1900)
A native of Massachusetts, he graduated first in his 1841 class at West Point and was posted to the Corps of Engineers. He was severely wounded in Virginia in August 1862. In July 1864 he returned to duty as superintendent of West Point but in September was sent to Nashville to strengthen the city's defenses. He remained in Nashville until the end of the war. He was brevetted major general in both the volunteer and regular forces. He is buried at Central Cemetery, Cohasset, Mass.

Key to Abbreviations:
k= killed
w= wounded
mw= mortally wounded
c= captured

Battle of Nashville Order of Battle • Confederate Army of Tennessee
Gen. John Bell Hood, Commanding

General John Bell Hood (1831-79)

Born in Kentucky and graduated from West Point in 1853, he gained fame as commander of the Texas Brigade at Gaines Mill, Va. and rapidly advanced in rank throughout the war. He fought at Second Manassas and Antietam and then led a division under Longstreet at Gettysburg, where his left arm was crippled. At Chickamauga in Georgia, he was badly wounded and his right leg amputated. Convalescing in Richmond, he cultivated his friendship with President Davis. A Corps commander in the Atlanta campaign, he succeeded Johnston as commander of the Army of Tennessee in July 1864. As was his nature, he immediately took the offensive, suffered consecutive defeats, and eventually surrendered Atlanta in Sept. 1864. Confounded at Spring Hill, Tenn. during his 1864 Tennessee offensive, he unwisely attacked Union fortifications at Franklin on Nov. 30, 1864 and suffered heavy losses. After the defeat at Nashville, he was relieved of command in Jan. 1865. After the war, he became a merchant and married, having 11 children in 10 years. He, his wife, and one child died of yellow fever in the epidemic of 1878. He is buried at Metairie Cemetery in New Orleans, La.

Stewart's Corps: Lt. Gen. Alexander P. Stewart

Lt. Gen. Alexander Peter Stewart (1821-1908)

Born in east Tennessee, he graduated West Point in 1842 and resigned in 1845 to become the chair of mathematics and philosophy at Cumberland College in Lebanon, Tenn. and at Nashville University. He was an anti-secessionist Whig who volunteered to fight for the South. Known as "Old Straight," he led a brigade in Polk's command in all battles of the Army of Tennessee until June 1864, when he assumed corps command upon Polk's death. He surrendered with Johnston in North Carolina in 1865. A businessman and educator, he served as Chancellor of the University of Mississippi from 1874-86 and was instrumental in establishing the Chattanooga-Chickamauga National Military Park. He is buried at St. Louis, Mo.

Loring's Division: Maj. Gen. William W. Loring
Featherston's Brigade: Brig. Gen. Winfield S. Featherston 1st, 3rd, 22nd, 31st, 33rd, 40th Mississippi; 1st Miss. Battalion
Adams's Brigade: Col. Robert Lowry 6th, 14th, 15th, 20th, 23rd, 43rd Mississippi
Scott's Brigade: Col. John Snodgrass 27th, 35th, 49th, 55th, 57th Alabama; 12th Louisiana
French's Division: Brig. Gen. Claudius Sears (w, c)
Ector's Brigade: Col. David Coleman 29th, 30th North Carolina; 9th Texas; 10th, 14th, 32nd Texas Cavalry
Cockrell's Brigade: Col. Peter C. Flournoy 1st, 2nd, 3rd, 4th, 5th, 6th Missouri; 1st Missouri Cavalry; 3rd Missouri Cavalry Battalion
Sears's Brigade: Lt. Col. Reuben H. Shotwell 4th, 35th, 36th, 39th, 46th Mississippi; 7th Mississippi Battalion
Walthall's Division: Maj. Gen. Edward C. Walthall
Quarles's Brigade: Brig. Gen. George D. Johnston 1st Alabama; 42nd, 46th, 48th, 49th, 53rd, 55th Tennessee
Canty's Brigade: Brig. Gen. Charles M. Shelley 17th, 26th, 29th Alabama; 37th Mississippi
Reynolds's Brigade: Brig. Gen. Daniel H. Reynolds 4th, 9th, 25th Arkansas; 1st, 2nd Arkansas Mounted Rifles

---

Lee's Corps: Lt. Gen. Stephen D. Lee

Lt. Gen. Stephen Dill Lee (1833-1908)

A native of South Carolina, he graduated from West Point in 1833. He served as an artillerist in the Eastern Theater through Sharpsburg and then commanded the Confederate artillery at Vicksburg, Miss. Captured there in July 1863, he was released months later and placed in command of cavalry in part of the Western Theater. The youngest lieutenant general in the CSA, he assumed command of Hood's Corps when Hood lead the Army of Tennessee. He served with Johnston in North Carolina when the war ended. He lived in Mississippi as a farmer, state senator, and the first president of Mississippi State University. He was a leading figure in the United Confederate Veterans. He is buried in Columbus, Miss.

Johnson's Division: Maj. Gen. Edward Johnson (c)
Deas's Brigade: Brig. Gen. Zachariah C. Deas 19th, 22nd, 25th, 38th, 50th Alabama
Manigault's Brigade: Lt. Col. William L. Butler 24th, 28th, 34th Alabama; 10th, 19th South Carolina
Sharp's Brigade: Brig. Gen. Jacob H. Sharp 7th, 9th, 10th, 41st, 44th Mississippi; 9th Battalion Miss. Sharpshooters
Brantley's Brigade: Brig. Gen. William F. Brantley 24th, 27th, 29th, 30th, 34th Mississippi; Dismounted Cavalry Company
Stevenson's Division: Maj. Gen. Carter L. Stevenson
Cummings's Brigade: Col. Elihu P. Watkins 24th, 36th, 39th, 56th Georgia
Pettus's Brigade: Brig. Gen. Edmund W. Pettus 20th, 23rd, 30th, 31st, 46th Alabama
Clayton's Division: Maj. Gen. Henry D. Clayton
Stovall's Brigade: Brig. Gen. Marcellus A. Stovall 40th, 41st, 42nd, 43rd, 52nd Georgia
Gibson's Brigade: Brig. Gen. Randall L. Gibson 1st, 4th, 13th, 16th, 19th, 20th, 25th, 30th Louisiana; 4th Louisiana Battalion; 14th Louisiana Battalion Sharpshooters
Holtzclaw's Brigade: Brig. Gen. James Holtzclaw 18th, 32nd, 36th, 38th, 58th Alabama

Battle of Nashville Order of Battle • Confederate Army of Tennessee
Gen. John Bell Hood, Commanding

Cheatham's Corps: Maj. Gen. Benjamin F. Cheatham

Major Gen. Benjamin Franklin Cheatham (1820-86)

A native Nashvillian, he served in the Mexican War as Colonel of the Tennessee Volunteers. While a farmer, he also served as Major General of the state militia. He commanded a brigade, division, then corps in the Army of Tennessee in every battle from Shiloh to Atlanta. Cheatham assumed command of Hardee's Corps as Hood began his 1864 Tennessee offensive. Blamed by Hood for the Union escape at Spring Hill, Tenn., Cheatham's Corps suffered heavily attacking fortifications the next day at Franklin. After the war, he ran unsuccessfully for Congress, and served as superintendent of state prisons and postmaster of Nashville. A hard fighter and hard drinker, he was universally beloved by his men. He is buried at Mt. Olivet Cemetery, Nashville.

Cleburne's Division: Brig. Gen. James A. Smith
Govan's Brigade: Brig. Gen. Daniel C. Govan 1st, 2nd, 5th, 6th, 7th, 8th, 13th, 15th, 19th, 24th Arkansas
Lowrey's Brigade: 16th, 33rd, 45th Alabama; 5th, 8th, 32nd Mississippi; 3rd Miss. Battalion
Granbury's Brigade: Capt. E.T. Broughton 5th Confederate; 35th Tennessee; 6th, 7th, 10th, 15th Texas; 17th, 18th, 24th, 25th Texas Cavalry; Nutt's Louisiana Cavalry
Smith's Brigade: Col. Charles H. Olmstead 54th, 57th, 63rd Georgia; 1st Georgia Volunteers

Brown's Division: Brig. Gen. Mark P. Lowrey
Gist's Brigade: Lt. Col. Zachariah L. Watters 46th, 65th Georgia; 2nd Battalion Ga. Sharpshooters; 16th, 24th South Carolina
Maney's Brigade: Col. Hume R. Feild 1st, 4th, 6th, 8th, 9th, 16th, 27th, 28th, 50th Tennessee
Strahl's Brigade: Col. Andrew J. Kellar 4th, 5th, 19th, 24th, 31st, 33rd, 38th, 41st Tennessee
Vaughan's Brigade: Col. William M. Watkins 11th, 12th, 13th, 29th, 47th, 51st, 52nd, 154th Tennessee

Bate's Division: Maj. Gen. William B. Bate
Tyler's Brigade: Brig. Gen. Thomas Benton Smith (w, c) 37th Georgia; 4th Battalion Ga. Sharpshooters; 2nd, 10th, 20th, 37th Tennessee
Finley's Brigade: Maj. Glover Ball 1st, 3rd, 4th, 6th, 7th Florida; 1st Florida Cavalry
Jackson's Brigade: Brig. Gen. Henry R. Jackson (c) 25th, 29th, 30th Georgia; 1st Ga. Confederate; 1st Battalion Georgia Sharpshooters

CAVALRY
Maj. Gen. Nathan Bedford Forrest

Major Gen. Nathan Bedford Forrest (1821-77)

Born in Bedford County, Tenn., he was a self-taught man, rising from poverty to millionaire planter and slave dealer in Memphis. He enlisted as a private in 1861 and equipped his own battalion of cavalry. He led his men out of Fort Donelson before its capture and served at Shiloh. He was promoted to brigadier general after he captured the garrison at Murfreesboro, Tenn. in July 1862. Known as the "Wizard of the Saddle," his cavalry exploits in the Union rear of the Western Theater caused much frustration on the part of U.S. Army commanders. His most brilliant victory was Brice's Crossroads, Miss.; his most controversial the capture of Fort Pillow, Tenn., known in the North as the Fort Pillow Massacre. His cavalry command destroyed the large Union supply depot at Johnsonville, Tenn. in Nov. 1864. Often contentious with superiors, he nevertheless commanded Hood's cavalry during the 1864 Tennessee offensive. He was detached to Murfreesboro during the Battle of Nashville and was stymied at the Battle of the Cedars. After the war, he again became a planter and managed a railroad. He was affiliated with the original Ku Klux Klan but resigned when it became too violent. He is buried at Forrest Park in Memphis, Tenn.

Chalmers's Division: Brig. Gen. James R. Chalmers
Rucker's Brigade: Col. Edmund W. Rucker (w, c) 7th Alabama; 5th Mississippi; 7th, 12th, 14th, 15th Tennessee; Forrest's Regiment Tennessee Cavalry
Biffle's Brigade: Col. Jacob B. Biffle 10th Tennessee

Buford's Division: Brig. Gen. Abraham Buford
Bell's Brigade: Col. Tyree H. Bell 2nd, 19th, 20th, 21st Tennessee; Nixon's Tennessee Regiment
Crossland's Brigade: Col. Edward Crossland 3rd, 7th, 8th, 12th Kentucky Mounted Infantry; 12th Kentucky; Huey's Kentucky Battalion

Jackson's Division: Brig. Gen. William H. Jackson
Armstrong's Brigade: Brig. Gen. Frank C. Armstrong 1st, 2nd, 28th Mississippi; Ballentine's Mississippi Regiment
Ross's Brigade: Brig. Gen. Lawrence S. Ross 5th, 6th, 9th Texas; 1st Texas Legion

Artillery: Morton's Tennessee Battery

Key to Abbreviations: k= killed w= wounded mw= mortally wounded c= captured

Battle of Nashville Order of Battle • Confederate Army of Tennessee
Gen. John Bell Hood, Commanding

ARTILLERY
Lee's Corps: Maj. John W. Johnston
Courtney's Battalion: Capt. James P. Douglas Dent's Alabama Battery; Douglas's Texas Battery; Garritty's Alabama Battery
Eldridge's Battalion: Capt. Charles E. Fenner Eufaula Alabama Battery; Fenner's Louisiana Battery; Stanford's Mississippi Battery
Johnson's Battalion: Capt. John B. Rowan Corput's Georgia Battery; Marshall's Tennessee Battery; Stephens's Light Artillery
Stewart's Corps: Lt. Col. Samuel C. Williams
Truehart's Battalion: Lumsden's Alabama Battery; Selden's Alabama Battery
Myrick's Battalion: Bouanchaud's Louisiana Battery; Cowan's Mississippi Battery; Darden's Mississippi Battery
Storrs's Battalion: Guiborps Missouri Battery; Hoskin's Mississippi Battery; Kolb's Alabama Battery
Cheatham's Corps: Col. Melancthon Smith
Hoxton's Battalion: Perry's Florida Battery; Phelan's Alabama Battery; Turner's Mississippi Battery
Hotchkiss's Battalion: Bledsoe's Missouri Battery; Goldtwaite's Alabama Battery; Key's Arkansas Battery
Cobb's Battalion: Ferguson's South Carolina Battery; Phillip's Tennessee Battery; Slocumb's Louisiana Battery

Gunpowder grinding wheels in Nashville's Centennial Park. Shipped through the Union blockade, these English-made wheels were used in Augusta, Ga. After the war, they were used at the Sycamore Powder Mills in Cheatham County, Tenn.

Rock City Guards & Nashville Militia

By the end of April 1861 there were 16 companies of volunteers drilling in Nashville, fearful they would not be ready in time to participate in the upcoming glorious, yet brief war against Northern aggression. There was Beauregard's Light Infantry, the Hickory Guards, the Hermitage Guards, Tennessee Rangers, Tennessee Rifles, Cheatham Rifles, and Harris Guards.

Formed two years prior and recognized by the Legislature as the city's official volunteer militia was the Rock City Guards, which boasted three companies of 100 men each. The eager volunteers drilled in the City Square, near the company headquarters at the Market House, and in Edgefield across the river. In April, the ladies of Nashville fashioned a flag for the Rock City Guards and presented it with these words, in part: "We place in your hand this flag that its folds may wave over you in the dark hour of conflict and recall to your minds the recollection that your mothers, your sisters and your children are praying at your firesides for your triumph and your safe return."

On May 3 at the State Capitol, the Rock City Guards were mustered into service as part of the First Tennessee Infantry Regiment of Volunteers.

After military training and drilling at Camp Harris in Allisonia and at Camp Cheatham in Springfield, the Rock City Guards returned to Nashville and camped on the lawn of the Nashville Female Academy and were greeted by wellwishers the next day at the train station.

On July 10, the Guards and the First Tennessee shipped out to Virginia. The regiment saw action in most of the battles of the Western Theater and returned to Nashville in December 1864 for their final desperate fighting.

Some of the Rock City Guards survived the war, but it was written in October 1863 that of the 300 men enlisting in the Rock City Guards more than two years earlier only about 25 were still alive.

⑳ Peach Orchard Hill

Some of the bloodiest fighting occurred at Peach Orchard Hill (Overton Hill) on the extreme right flank of the Confederate army the second day of the Battle of Nashville.

The U.S. Army suffered 1,000 casualties (one-third of its total in the battle) during several ill-fated assaults against heavily fortified Confederate positions under Gen. Stephen D. Lee. The 13th Regiment of the U.S. Colored Troops did reach the parapet but lost 220 men in heavy fighting.

Due to highway construction, little remains of the hill, which was part of the Overton estate known as Travellers Rest (Site No. 21).

㉑ Travellers Rest Plantation and Museum

Built in 1799, Travellers Rest at 636 Farrell Parkway was the home of Judge John Overton, a member of the state Supreme Court. The house began as a two-story, four-room Federal-style clapboard structure with additions built in 1808, 1828, and 1887. Today, the home is furnished in the period of the lifetime of Judge Overton, who died in 1833.

At the beginning of the Civil War, the home was occupied by Overton's widow (she died in 1862), her son John and his wife Harriet and their children. The farm, worked by 80 slaves, covered 1,050 acres and was valued at $68 million (in today's dollars). When the Union occupied Nashville in February 1862, John Overton fled his home to avoid arrest and imprisonment. Appointed to the rank of colonel by the governor before the war, Overton offered considerable financial support to the Confederate army.

Confederate Gen. John Bell Hood arrived from Franklin on Dec. 2, 1864 and made Travellers Rest his headquarters. From here, he directed the building of a five-mile defensive line south of the Union-occupied city. Also here, he met on Dec. 8 with Gen. Benjamin Franklin Cheatham, who offered his apologies for miscommunications which allowed the Federal army to escape at Spring Hill on Nov. 29.

At Travellers Rest, Mrs. John Overton hosted a dinner attended by Gen. Hood and five other generals following the marriage of one of Hood's staff officers.

During the Battle of Nashville, the women and children huddled nervously in the cellar awaiting the outcome, Gen. Hood having relocated his headquarters to the west. The Confederate lines collapsed and the retreating army moved past the house, followed by Union soldiers. On the night of Dec. 16, Union Gen. W.L. Elliott slept in the same bedroom occupied earlier by Hood.

Travellers Rest is owned by the Colonial Dames of America in Tennessee and is listed on the National Register of Historic Places.

Travellers Rest is located at 636 Farrell Parkway, Nashville, TN 37220. Call (615) 832-8197.

Admission is charged. Group rates are available.

Hours are Mon.-Sat., 10-4:00; Sun., 1-4:00. Closed most major holidays.

A house tour is offered that covers the time period of the battle.

A brochure, "Civil War Walking Tour on the Grounds of Travellers Rest," is available.

22 Stewart's Stone Wall

A Metro Historical Commission marker at 4616 Lealand Lane marks the stone wall behind which fought Major Gen. William Loring's division of Stewart's Corps, on Dec. 16, 1864. All Federal attacks were beaten back until the Confederate line was broken a mile to the west. The division retreated south through the hills toward Brentwood.

23 Shy's Hill

On the second day of battle, Shy's Hill (known as Compton Hill at the time) was a formidable position occupied by Gen. William Bate's division of Cheatham's Corps on the extreme left flank. Although positioned 600 yards from the hill, the Federals of the XXIII Corps and XVI Corps remained mostly dormant until 4:15 p.m. when Gen. John McArthur ordered McMillen's Brigade to "take that hill." The subsequent charge up the hill resulted in the rout of the entire Confederate army in one of the most decisive battles of the war. Col. William Shy of the 20th Tennessee defended the hill to the last, shot in the forehead at point-blank range. Gen. Thomas Benton Smith was captured here.

At the top of the hill visitors can see traces of the Confederate earthworks, which were erroneously positioned higher than the military crest. At the time of the battle, the hill, like much of the countryside, had been cleared of trees.

Congressional Medal of Honor - Battle of Nashville

The Congressional Medal of Honor (to recognize "gallantry in action") was awarded to 19 Union soldiers and sailors who fought in the Battle of Nashville:

ANDERSON, MARION T.
Captain, Company D, 51st Indiana Infantry.
Entered service at: Kokomo, Ind.
Birthplace: Decatur County, Ind.
Date of issue: 1 September 1893.
Citation: On Dec. 16, he led his regiment over five lines of the enemy's works, where he fell, severely wounded.

CARR, FRANKLIN
Corporal, Company D, 124th Ohio Infantry.
Birthplace: Stark County, Ohio.
Date of issue: 24 February 1865.
Citation: Recapture of U.S. guidon from a rebel battery on Dec. 16.

CHURCHILL, SAMUEL J.
Corporal, Co. G, 2d Illinois Light Artillery.
Entered service at DeKalb County, Ill.
Birthplace: Rutland County, Vt.
Date of issue: 20 January 1897.
Citation: On Dec. 15, when the fire of the enemy's batteries compelled the men of his detachment for a short time to seek shelter, he stood manfully at his post and for some minutes worked his gun alone.

COLWELL, OLIVER
First Lieutenant, Co. G, 95th Ohio Infantry.
Birthplace: Champaign County, Ohio.
Date of issue: 24 February 1865.
Citation: Capture of flag on Dec. 16.

DITZENBACK, JOHN
Quartermaster, U.S. Navy.
Born: 1828, New York, N.Y.
Accredited to: Indiana. G.O. No.: 59, 22 June 1865.
Citation: Served on board the U.S. Monitor Neosho during the engagement with enemy batteries at Bells Mills, Cumberland River, near Nashville, Tenn., 6 December 1864. Carrying out his duties courageously during the engagement, Ditzenback gallantly left the pilot house after the flag and signal staffs of that vessel had been shot away and, taking the flag which was drooping over the wheelhouse, made it fast to the stump of the highest mast remaining, although the ship was still under a heavy fire from the enemy.

FERRELL, JOHN H.
Pilot, U.S. Navy.
Entered service at: Illinois. Born: 15 April 1823, Tennessee. G.O. No.: 59, 22 June 1865.
Citation: Served on board the U.S. Monitor Neosho during the engagement with enemy batteries at Bells Mills, Cumberland River, near Nashville, Tenn., 6 December 1864. Carrying out his duties courageously during the engagement, Ferrell gallantly left the pilothouse after the flag and signal staffs of that vessel had been shot away and, taking the flag which was drooping over the wheelhouse, make it fast to the stump of the highest mast remaining although the ship was still under a heavy fire from the enemy.

GARRETT, WILLIAM
Sergeant, Company G, 41st Ohio Infantry.
Birthplace: England.
Date of issue: 24 February 1865.
Citation: With several companions dashed forward Dec. 16, the first to enter the enemy's works, taking possession of 4 pieces of artillery and captured the flag of the 13th Mississippi Infantry (C.S.A.).

GERE, THOMAS P.
First Lieutenant and Adjutant, 5th Minnesota Infantry.
Birthplace: Chemung County, N.Y.
Date of issue: 24 February 1865.
Citation: Capture of flag of 4th Mississippi (C.S.A.) on Dec. 16.

KALTENBACH, LUTHER
Corporal, Company F, 12th Iowa Infantry.
Entered service at: Honey Creek, Iowa.
Birthplace: Germany.
Date of issue: 24 February 1865.
Citation: Capture of flag of 44th Mississippi Infantry (C.S.A.) on Dec. 16.

MAY, WILLIAM
Private, Company H, 32d Iowa Infantry.
Entered service at: Maysville, Franklin Co., Iowa.
Birthplace: Pennsylvania.
Date of issue: 24 February 1865.
Citation: Ran ahead of his regiment over the enemy's works Dec. 16 and captured from its bearer the flag of Bonanchad's Confederate battery (C.S.A.).

McCLEARY, CHARLES H.
First Lieutenant, Co. C. 72d Ohio Infantry.
Birthplace: Sandusky County, Ohio.
Date of issue: 24 February 1865.
Citation: Capture of flag of 4th Florida Infantry (C.S.A.) on Dec. 16, while in advance of his lines.

MOORE, WILBUR F.
Private, Company C, 117th Illinois Infantry.

Entered service at: Lebanon, St. Clair Co., Ill.
Birthplace: Lebanon, St. Clair County, Ill.
Date of issue: 22 February 1865.
Citation: Captured flag of a Confederate battery while far in advance of the Union lines Dec. 16.

PARKS, JAMES W.
Corporal, Company F, 11th Missouri Infantry.
Entered service at: Xenia, Clay County, Ill.
Birthplace: Lawrence County, Ohio.
Date of issue: 24 February 1865.
Citation: Capture of flag on Dec. 16.

POST, PHILIP SIDNEY
Colonel, 59th Illinois Infantry.
Place and date: At Nashville, Tenn., 15-16 December 1864.
Entered service at: Galesburg, Ill.
Birth: 19 March 1833, Flordia, Orange Co., N.Y.
Date of issue: 18 March 1893.
Citation: Led his brigade in an attack upon a strong position under a terrific fire of grape, canister, and musketry; was struck down by a grapeshot after he had reached the enemy's works.

SIMMONS, WILLIAM T.
Lieutenant, Co. C, 11th Missouri Infantry.
Birth: 29 January 1843, Green County, Ill.
Date of issue: 24 February 1865.
Citation: Capture of flag of 34th Alabama Infantry (C.S.A) on Dec. 16. Being the first to enter the works, he shot and wounded the enemy color bearer.

SLOAN, ANDREW J.
Private, Company H, 12th Iowa Infantry.
Entered service at: Colesburg, Delaware County, Iowa.
Birthplace: Bedford County, Pa.
Date of issue: 24 February 1865.
Citation: Captured flag of 1st Louisiana Battery (C.S.A.) on Dec. 16.

SMITH, OTIS W.
Private, Company G, 95th Ohio Infantry.
Birth: Logan County, Ohio.
Date of issue: 24 February 1865.
Citation: Capture of flag of 6th Florida Infantry (C.S.A.) on Dec. 16.

STOKES, GEORGE
Private, Company C, 122d Illinois Infantry.
Entered service at: Jerseyville, Ill.
Birthplace: England.
Date of issue: 24 February 1865.
Citation: Capture of flag on Dec. 16.

WELCH, GEORGE W.
Private, Company A, 11th Missouri Infantry.
Entered service at: Keokuk, Lee County, Iowa.
Birthplace: Brown County, Iowa.
Date of issue: 24 February 1965
Citation: Captured the flag of the 13th Alabama Infantry (C.S.A.) on Dec. 16.

㉔ Majestic Belle Meade "Queen of Tennessee Plantations"

Belle Meade in southwest Davidson County is known as the "Queen of Tennessee Plantations." In the 1800s the 5,400-acre estate was a world-renown thoroughbred horse nursery and stud farm. It was the home to Iroquois, the first American-bred horse to win the English Derby.

In 1807, Virginian John Harding bought 250 acres and a log cabin known as Dunham Station, a trading post on the Natchez Trace. Several years later the farm gained reputation as a stud farm when the famed horse Imp. Boaster stood as stud there. The original house was probably begun in the 1820s.

In 1853 John Harding's son, William Giles Harding, completed the Greek Revival mansion, doubling its size and adding the front porch and columns, which are solid limestone.

Harding was very wealthy and very pro-secession and donated $500,000 to the Southern cause. When the Federals occupied Nashville in February 1862, Harding was arrested and sent north to Fort Mackinac in Michigan to be imprisoned. His wife, Elizabeth I. McGavock, was left to tend their farm in his absence. In September, Harding was released on parole and returned to Belle Meade.

Belle Meade was headquarters to Confederate Gen. James R. Chalmers of Gen. Nathan Bedford Forrest's cavalry command prior to the Battle of Nashville in December 1864.

On the first day of the battle, Union soldiers burned the Confederate wagons parked at the racetrack while Chalmers was elsewhere. Returning to Belle Meade, Chalmers' men charged the Union soldiers and drove them back before running into an enemy infantry camp. The Northerners fired as the Confederate cavalry galloped back past the mansion, where Selene Harding, 19, waved a handkerchief despite the bullets flying around her. Bullet holes can still be seen in the porch columns.

After the war, William Harding turned over control of the farm to his son-in-law, William Jackson, a West Point graduate who had commanded a cavalry division under Gen. S.D. Lee in Mississippi and Louisiana.

Under Jackson's tutelage, Belle Meade (French for "beautiful meadow") became an internationally renown thoroughbred farm and showplace. The farm sold breeding stock of ponies, Alderney cattle, Cotswold sheep, and Cashmere goats. The vast estate also featured a 600-acre deer park.

At its sale in 1904, Belle Meade was the oldest and largest thoroughbred farm in the nation.

Belle Meade Plantation remained a private residence until 1953, when it was sold to the state. The historical site is now maintained by the Association for the Preservation of Tennessee Antiquities.

Today, the National Historic Place covers 30 acres and includes the Greek Revival mansion, the huge carriage house and stables, the smokehouse, garden house, creamery, and the original 1790 log cabin.

Tours are conducted by docents in period costume following an informative video. The Wills Reception Center also features a large gift shop.

Belle Meade Plantation is located at 5025 Harding Rd., Nashville, TN 37205. Call (615) 356-0501 or (800) 270-3991. Admission fee charged. Open Mon.-Sat., 9-5; Sun., 1-5. Last tour at 4 p.m. Closed Thanksgiving, Christmas, and New Year's.

25 Kelley's Point

The U.S.S. Neosho *engages Confederate batteries at Bell's Bend on the Cumberland River west of Nashville on Dec. 6, 1864.*

The largest sustained battle between Confederate cavalry and the Union "brown water" navy occurred at Bell's Bend in the Cumberland River, nine miles west of Nashville, during the two weeks before the Battle of Nashville.

On the river bank, four artillery pieces under the command of Lt. Col. David C. Kelley effectively blocked the Cumberland River against seven heavily armed Union gunboats from Dec. 2-15, 1864. Confederate cavalry and Federal gunboats clashed in six separate engagements.

During the fourth engagement, on Dec. 6, 1864, the *U.S.S. Neosho* was hit more than 100 times by cannon fire without sinking. The ironclad narrowly avoided disaster when an unexploded Confederate shell breached the ship's iron plating and lodged in its powder magazine.

Pilot John Ferrell and quartermaster John Ditzenback were later awarded the Congressional Medal of Honor for saving the Union colors aboard the *Neosho* when the flag was shot away by Confederate gunfire.

Fortunately for the Federals, troops under Gen. Andrew Jackson Smith arrived from Missouri by steamboat just one day prior to the Confederate "blockade."

Nashville was one of the largest Civil War battlefields in geographical size. From Bell's Bend in the west to the Confederate positions on the Tennessee & Chattanooga Railroad in the east was a distance of 14 miles.

Today, six acres of Kelley's Point Battlefield are preserved and interpreted as part of the city's Brookmeade Park greenway. The Battle of Nashville Preservation Society was instrumental in saving the riverside site, which is surrounded by recent commercial development.

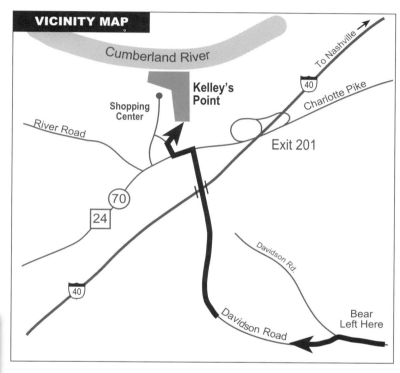

A tugboat pushes barges on the Cumberland River at Bell's Bend.

Aftermath

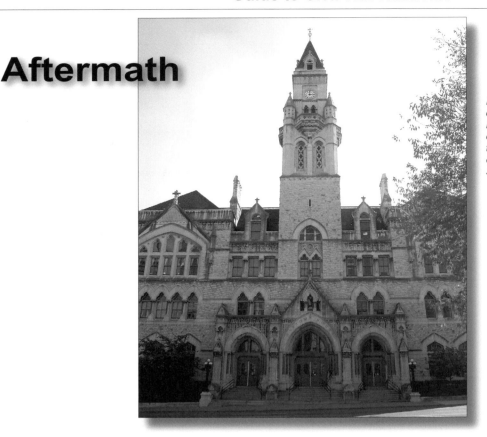

In a symbolic gesture to signal the end of Reconstruction in the South, President Rutherford B. Hayes laid the cornerstone of the U.S. Customs House during a visit to Nashville on Sept. 19, 1877. This grand example of Victorian Gothic architecture stands at 701 Broadway.

On April 10, 1865, a week after the fall of Richmond, Va., news arrived in Nashville of Lee's surrender to Grant. Crowds gathered in the city to read special bulletins, and the legislature celebrated and then adjourned for the day.

On Fri., April 14 cannons were fired from every post in the Department of the Cumberland to honor the raising of Old Glory over Fort Sumter. Sat., April 15 was proclaimed as a day of thanksgiving and rejoicing. Of course, it was the Unionists in Nashville who were doing all the rejoicing. According to plans, at 10 am., businesses would close, followed by a parade of 15,000 soldiers led by Gens. Thomas, Rousseau, and Miller and music by all the military bands. From Fort Negley the soldiers would march to the Public Square, where they would pass in review. Fireworks and a military band concert would follow.

As the troops formed for the Saturday parade, telegrams arrived announcing the assassination of President Abraham Lincoln in Washington. The crowds were stunned into silence. The celebration was immediately canceled. Soldiers returned to their barracks as the bands played funeral dirges. Colorful bunting on the buildings was replaced with black crepe. Citizens were amazed to learn that the assassin was actor John Wilkes Booth, who had performed at the Nashville Theater in early 1864.

Six or seven citizens who rejoiced at the news of Lincoln's death were shot, bayoneted, or mauled to death by Union soldiers.

Upon Lincoln's death, newly inaugurated Vice President Andrew Johnson, formerly the military governor of Tennessee, became the 17th U.S. President. He called for a national day of mourning on Wednesday, April 19.

On that day, all Nashville businesses were closed, flags were flown at half-mast, and all military posts fired a 21-gun salute. At 10 a.m., church bells tolled and a huge funeral procession began to thread its way through the city. The cortege, consisting of 40,000 civilians and 8,000 troops, began at Fort Negley and progressed to the Public Square, the Capitol, and then out Harding Pike to an open field set up for public speakers. The procession included a three-tiered catafalque covered in black fabric and topped by an American flag. The coffin-laden platform was drawn by 12 horses, six black and six white, alternating in color.

Weeks later, on May 8, the U.S. Army Fourth Corps of 20,000 troops passed in review of Gen. Thomas in a field at the south edge of Nashville. Reportedly it was the largest troop review in the Western Theater. The following day, down south in Alabama, Gen. Forrest surrendered his remaining command. The war was over.

Fourteen months later, Tennessee, the last state to leave the Union, became the first Confederate state to be readmitted into the Union. Tennessee also had been the first state to ratify the 13th Amendment, which abolished slavery.

Beyond Nashville: Murfreesboro

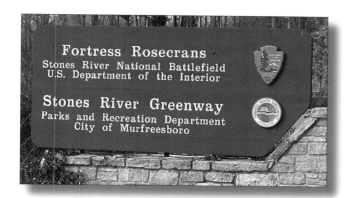

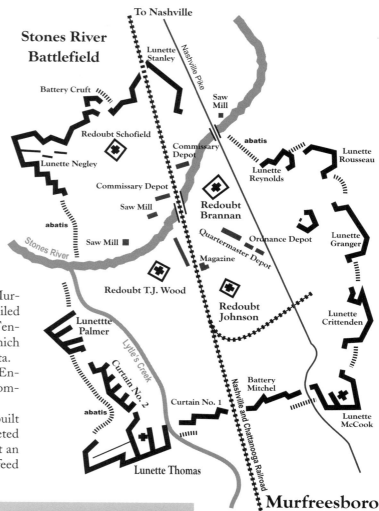

Huge railroad depot built in Murfreesboro to support 1863-64 Union campaigns

In the months following the Battle of Stones River near Murfreesboro, thousands of Union soldiers and black laborers toiled around the clock to build a huge fortified supply depot on the Tennessee & Chattanooga Railroad, named Fortress Rosecrans, which would supply future campaigns against Chattanooga and Atlanta.

It was designed by Brig. Gen. James St. Clair Morton, Chief Engineer of the Army of the Cumberland and named after the commanding general, William Rosecrans.

The construction of the fort, the largest earthen fortification built during the Civil War, began on Jan. 23, 1863 and was completed in June. The resulting 200-acre fort was large enough to protect an army of 50,000 troops and could stockpile enough supplies to feed the army for up to 90 days.

A vast complex of weapons, ammunition, and food storehouses sprawled across the open ground within the fort. The fort also included four sawmills and a 50-acre vegetable garden used by the large local hospital.

In addition to 14,600 feet of exterior defenses—ten lunettes linked by curtain walls and other obstructions—Fortress Rosecrans included four interior fortifications, called redoubts.

Only a few sections of the fortress complex exist today—Curtain Wall #2 and Lunettes Palmer and Thomas in Old Fort Park, and Redoubt Brannan along the Old Nashville Pike.

Redoubt Brannan, named for Gen. John M. Brannan, chief of artillery for the Army of the Cumberland, commands a view of the railroad bridge over the Stones River and the Nashville Turnpike. It is accessible from the Stones River Greenway.

By the end of 1863, more than 50 cannon stood ready to defend Fortress Rosecrans. One battery in Lunette Thomas was trained on the Rutherford County Courthouse 1,770 yards away. The Federals threatened to shell the town if the Confederates attacked the fort.

Fortress Rosecrans is located in Old Fort Park off Hwy. 96 (Old Fort Parkway) in Murfreesboro. The site is free and open daily. There is an 0.6-mile interpretive trail with signage. For more information, call (615) 893-9501. The fortress site is connected to the Stones River National Battlefield by the Stones River Greenway.

> "We did not enlist to get a job of working. We expected just a big picnic with good clothes, good rations, regular pay and glory, not work and mud."
>
> **Lyman S. Widney**
> **34th Illinois Infantry**

Imposing fort in Franklin protected vital railroad crossing

Fort Granger, a Union earthwork fortification, was built in March-May 1863 to guard the railroad bridge over the Harpeth River near Franklin.

Named for Gen. Gordon Granger, commander of Federal forces in Franklin in 1863, this earthen fort was constructed by laborers working 24 hours a day under the supervision of Col. W.E. Merrill of the U.S. Topographical Engineers.

Figuer's Bluff was chosen as the site for the fort because it held command over the southern and northern approaches to Franklin and held military control over the Harpeth River bridge of the Tennessee & Alabama Railroad.

Fort Granger was 781 feet long and 346 feet wide, encompassing 11.76 acres and contained two fortified fronts on the northern and eastern sides.

By April 1863, Fort Granger held 18 field guns and two 30-pound siege cannons. At full capacity, the fort could house 5,194 infantry troops, 2,728 cavalry, and 24 artillery pieces.

During the war, Fort Granger was attacked several times by Confederate cavalry units.

Shells from the fort landed in some Franklin houses during the Battle of Franklin on Nov. 30, 1864, during which it served as the final headquarters for Gen. John M. Schofield. During that engagement the fort held 8,500 soldiers and 24 pieces of artillery.

The powder magazine at Fort Granger was made from the basement of a house which stood on the site before the war. It was lined with bricks from the nearby Harpeth Academy, which at that time stood west of Hillsboro Pike.

The magazine was capable of holding 1,200 rounds of artillery ammunition. In 1864, a shed was built over the magazine to keep the ammunition dry. The ammunition was frequently taken out and aired because of dampness.

The cavalier, or fort within a fort, was built in the southernmost area where the ground was the highest. This was the strongest area of Fort Granger and, in case of overwhelming attack, the place where defenders would make a final stand. This was an ideal location for artillery and provided the best view of the surrounding area.

Captain Giles J. Cockerill's Battery D, 1st Ohio Light Artillery, fired 163 rounds from its guns located in this area during the Battle of Franklin. The fort's artillery inflicted serious damage on the right wing of the Confederate Army of Tennessee, Loring's Division, which attacked along the railroad cut.

Long neglected after the Civil War, Fort Granger was purchased by the City of Franklin in the 1970s. It can be accessed from the rear portion of Pinkerton City Park off Hwy. 96 between Franklin and I-65 South. The fort is open daily and free of charge. There is interpretive signage and an overlook of the city but no other facilities. Only the earthenworks remain today.

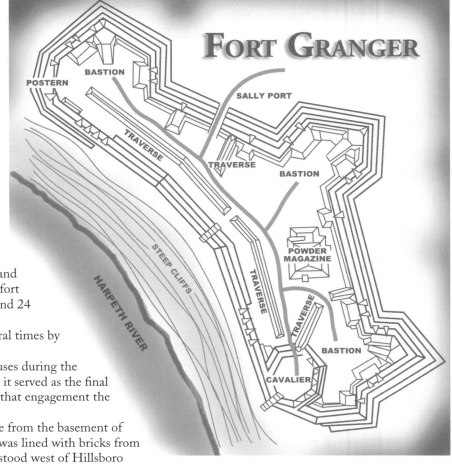

Civil War Sites in Middle Tennessee

Information about Civil War sites in Middle Tennessee, easily accessible from Nashville. For information, call the listed phone numbers. Brochures for many of these sites are available at the Nashville Visitors Center or on the Internet.

Chattanooga

Chickamauga and Chattanooga National Military Park
P.O. Box 2128, Fort Oglethorpe, GA 30742
Call (706) 866-9241.
Point Park on Lookout Mountain and Visitors Center. Historic Cravens House. Reservations along Missionary Ridge. Orchard Knob Reservation. National Cemetery. Several local Civil War museums. Chickamauga Battlefield driving tour. Hiking trails and horse riding trails.

Clarksville

Fort Defiance/Fort Bruce
200 South 2nd St., Clarksville, TN 37040
Earthen fortifications
Free, open daily. For tours, call the Clarksville-Montgomery Co. Museum at (615) 648-5780.

Columbia-Mt. Pleasant

Athenaeum Rectory
808 Athenaeum St., Columbia, TN 38401
Call (615) 381-4822
Antebellum school, museum, gift shop
Open Feb. thru Dec.; Tues-Sat., 10-4; Sun., 1-4
Admission fee.

St. John's Episcopal Church
Hwy. 243, Mt. Pleasant, TN
Call Maury County Visitors Bureau at 1-888-852-1860
Antebellum plantation church
Church closed, but grounds open to public.

Rattle & Snap Plantation
Rt. 1, Box 130, 1522 N. Main St.,
Columbia, TN 38401
Call (800) 258-3875; (615) 379-5861
Antebellum mansion.

Dover

Ft. Donelson National Battlefield
P.O. Box 434, Dover, TN 37058
Call (615) 232-5706
National battlefield, visitors center, driving tour, cemetery.
Free admission. Open daily, 8-4:30.

Dover Hotel (Surrender House)
P.O. Box 434, Dover, TN 37058
Call (615) 232-5348.
Free admission. Open June thru Sept., noon-4.

Eva

Nathan B. Forrest State Park
Star Route, Eva, TN 38333
Call (901) 584-6356.
Historic Sites, Museum, Folklife Center.
Free admission. Park open daily.
Museum open April thru Nov., 8-4:30.

Franklin

The Carter House
1140 Columbia Ave., Franklin, TN
Call (615) 791-1861.
Antebellum mansion (pictured above), visitors center, museum, video, gift shop. Interpretive center for Battle of Franklin. Admission fee; group rates available.
Open April through October, Mon. thru Sat., 9-5; Sun., 1-5.
Open Nov. through March, Mon. thru Sat., 9-4; Sunday, 1-4.

Carnton Plantation
1345 Carnton Lane, Franklin, TN 37064
Call (615) 794-0903
Antebellum mansion, museum, gift shop, cemetery
Admission fee; group rates available.
Open April through October: Mon. thru Sat., 9-5; Sun., 1-5.
Open Nov. through March: Mon. thru Sat., 9-4; Sunday, 1-4.

Winstead Hill
Columbia Avenue (Hwy. 31 South)
Memorial park open daily to the public, free.

Fort Granger
Located at Pinkerton Park.
Mailing address: P.O. Box 305, Franklin, TN 37065
Hwy. 96, Franklin, TN
Historic fortifications with interpretive signage.
Open daily, 8-5, to public; no admission fee.

Historic Downtown Franklin
Downtown Franklin Association
P.O. Box 807, Franklin, TN 37065
Call (615) 790-7094.
19th Century town square, Confederate statue, 15-block historic district.

Hartsville

Battle of Hartsville Driving Tour
Battle of Hartsville Preservation
105 East Main St., Hartsville, TN 37074
Call (615) 374-9243.
Driving tour of 17 sites of Battle of Hartsville (Dec. 7, 1862).
Free admission. Open daily.
Brochure available from Hartsville Chamber of Commerce at Trousdale County Courthouse, 200 E. Main St.
Office open Mon.-Fri., 8:30-4:30.

New Johnsonville

Johnsonville State Historic Area
Rt. 1, P.O. Box 37-4
New Johnsonville, TN 37134
Call (615) 535-2789
Museum (open by appointment only), fortifications.
Free admission. Open daily, 8-sunset

Murfreesboro

Stones River National Battlefield
3501 Old Nashville Hwy.
Murfreesboro, TN 37129
Call (615) 893-9501.
National battlefield, cemetery, museum, bookstore, Hazen Monument (pictured above), oldest Civil War monument.
Free admission. Open daily, 8-5. Closed Christmas Day.

Fortress Rosecrans
3501 Old Nashville Hwy.
Murfreesboro, TN 37129
Call (615) 893-9501
Remains of fortifications. Part of Stones River National Battlefield system.
Free admission. Open daily.

Oaklands Historic Home
900 North Maney Ave.
Murfreesboro, TN 37130
Call (615) 893-0022.
Antebellum mansion, museum, gift shop.
Admission fee. Open Tues.-Sat., 10-4; Sun., 1-4.

Shiloh

Shiloh National Military Park
Rt. 1, P.O. Box 9, Shiloh, TN 38376
Call (901) 689-5275.
National battlefield, cemetery, museum, bookstore.
Admission fee. Open daily, 8-5.

Smyrna

Sam Davis Home
1399 Sam Davis Rd., Smyrna, TN 37167
Call (615) 459-2341.
Historic home, museum, guided tour, video, gift shop.
Admission fee.
Open June thru Aug.: Mon.-Sat., 9-5; Sun., 1-5.
Sept. thru May: Mon.-Sat., 10-4; Sun., 1-4.

Spring Hill

Rippavilla Plantation
5700 Main Street, Spring Hill, TN 37174
Call (615) 486-9037 or (800) 381-1865.
Guided tours, museum, gift shop.
Admission fee.
Open April thru Oct.: Mon.-Sat., 9-5; Sun., 1-5.
Nov. thru March: Mon.-Sat., 9-4; Sun., 1-4.

Tennessee Antebellum Trail
5700 Main Street, Spring Hill, TN 37174
Call (615) 486-9037 or (800) 381-1865.
Headquartered at Rippavilla Plantation.
Free brochure available by phone or at address above.
Self-driving 90-mile tour includes 55 Civil War sites, and nine antebellum homes open to public. Discount ticket available for nine home sites. Includes listings for accommodations, dining, and shops.

Tullahoma

Tullahoma Campaign Trail
300 South Jackson St.
Tullahoma, TN 37388
Call (800) 799-6131 or (931) 454-9446.
Free brochure available at phone or address above. Self-driving, 130-mile tour of Civil War sites open to public (unless private property). Sites include Hoovers Gap, Fairfield, Wartrace, Bell Buckle, Liberty Gap, Tullahoma, Manchester, Winchester, Cowan, Shelbyville, Sewanee.

Selected Bibliography and Suggested Reading

Atlas to Accompany the Official Records of the Union and Confederate Armies, Washington, D.C., 1891-95.

Blue & Gray Magazine, "The Battle of Nashville" Vol. XI, Issue 2, December 1993.

Boatner, Mark M., III, *The Civil War Dictionary.* Vintage Books. New York. 1991.

Brumbaugh, Thomas B., Strayhorn, Martha I., and Gore, Gary G., editors, *Architecture of Middle Tennessee,* Vanderbilt University Press, 1974.

Bucy, Carole S. and Kaplan, Carol F., *The Nashville City Cemetery: History Carved in Stone,* Nashville City Cemetery Association, Inc., 2000.

Connelly, Thomas L., *Civil War Tennessee: Battles and Leaders,* University of Tennessee Press, 1979.

Durham, Walter T., *Nashville: The Occupied City,* Tennessee Historical Society, 1985.

Durham, Walter T., *Reluctant Partners: Nashville and the Union,* Tennessee Historical Society, 1987.

Echoes of Glory: Illustrated Atlas of the Civil War. Time-Life Books. Alexandria, VA. 1991.

Groom, Winston, *Shrouds of Glory, From Atlanta to Nashville: The Last Great Campaign of the Civil War,* Atlantic Monthly Press, 1995.

Hoobler, James A., *Cities Under the Gun: Images of Occupied Nashville and Chattanooga,* Rutledge Hill Press, 1986.

Horn, Stanley F., *The Decisive Battle of Nashville,* Louisiana State University Press, 1956.

Logsdon, David R., *Eyewitnesses at the Battle of Nashville.* Kettle Mills Press. Nashville. 2004.

McDonough, James Lee, *Nashville: The Western Confederacy's Final Gamble,* University of Tennessee Press, 2004.

Official Guide to Civil War Discovery Trail. Civil War Preservation Trust. Simon & Schuster Macmillan Co., New York. 1998.

A Path Divided: Tennessee's Civil War Heritage Trail. Tennessee Wars Commission. Nashville. 2000.

Sword, Wiley, *The Confederacy's Last Hurrah: Spring Hill, Franklin and Nashville.* University Press of Kansas. 1992.

Tennessee: The Civil War Years. Tennessee 200, Inc. 1996.

Tennessee Historical Markers. Tennessee Historical Commission. 1996.

Wardin, Albert W., Jr., *Belmont Mansion,* Belmont Mansion Association, 1989.

Warner, Ezra W., *Generals in Blue,* Louisiana State University Press, 1964.

Warner, Ezra W., *Generals in Gray,* Louisiana State University Press, 1959.

Watkins, Sam R., *Co. Aytch: A Confederate Memoir of the Civil War.* Simon & Schuster. 1962.